BLAZING TRAILS

Stories of guidance for women to succeed in the business world on their own terms

BLAZING TRAILS

A lifetime of speaking up, standing out, and staying true to myself

LEVONNE LOUIE

Citrine PRESS

Citrine Press
Suite 2202, 1078 6th Avenue SW
Calgary, AB
Canada T2P 5N6

Cataloguing data available from Library and Archives Canada
ISBN 978-0-9938037-4-1 (paperback)
ISBN 978-0-9938037-5-8 (ebook)

Produced by Page Two
www.pagetwo.com

Editing by Lana Okerlund
Cover design by Peter Cocking and Taysia Louie
Interior design by Taysia Louie

www.levonnelouie.com

This book is dedicated to my daughter, Megan.
Your love, encouragement, and support
inspire me to be the best that I can be. I am
so proud to see you blaze your own trail.

_____

CONTENTS

INTRODUCTION

I T HAS TAKEN me a while to own the title of trailblazer. This word has been attributed to me more than a few times as I conclude my career in the oil and gas industry. Women have come up to me at various events and called me a trailblazer because I reached an executive level as vice president of land, first at a junior company and later at an intermediate exploration and production company. They have said I am a trailblazer for the way I understand the technical aspects of the industry, the negotiations that occur, and the bigger strategic picture. People have also talked about the ways I give back, both to the oil and gas industry and to my community.

Some of my younger cousins have called me a trailblazer as the first member of my direct and extended family to be employed in the oil and gas industry. I was also one of the first in our large extended family to divorce and to raise a child as a single mom while working full-time in a profession.

These people seem to see me as an example of what can be achieved by someone who has worked from the ground up. I have had men tell me that they hope their young daughters can achieve what I have achieved.

Often when people call me a trailblazer, I am uncomfortable, because I don't see myself as having done anything special. I just pursued things I was interested in, and then later in my career I felt a need to give back. It always surprises me to hear of the impact that my actions or words may have had on someone else.

I am writing this book based on my close to forty years of experience working in the oil and gas industry in Calgary, the oil capital of Canada and a city known for its entrepreneurial, pioneering spirit.

While, on the surface, the oil and gas industry appears to be very diverse in terms of gender, it has traditionally been and still remains very male-dominated, particularly at the management, executive, and board levels. The technical roles tend to be held mostly by men and the administrative roles tend to be held mostly by women. While there has been much progress in bringing women into the science, technical, and engineering domains, there are still many more men than women in these areas, particularly when you start moving up the management levels.

As Deborah Yedlin noted in the *Calgary Herald* (December 28, 2017), there is a "dearth of women in senior positions and on corporate boards... Of the women who have climbed to the top, the majority are in what would be termed pink ghetto functions such as corporate services and human resources. You are hard pressed to find women in senior positions with operating and front-line responsibilities: yes, there is something called occupational segregation. And that's even when they have the iron ring of an engineer."

Oil and gas companies in Canada are also not very ethnically diverse when you look up the management ladder. Unless the company is based in a foreign country such as China, there is relatively little ethnic diversity at the management and executive levels.

Is it a matter of like hiring and promoting? Are white males more comfortable hiring and promoting other white males because they understand them and can relate to them better? Even though there is a lot of discussion today about increasing diversity, I have not seen much change in the upper levels of the oil and gas industry in Calgary over the past forty years.

The lack of gender and ethnic diversity brings the threat of a singular point of view and stagnation. When the majority of the people around the leadership or boardroom table have the same background and experience, it is easy for groupthink to occur. I have seen many instances when those who offer a different opinion, be they men or women, are shut down or ignored. In the case of women offering a different idea or approach, I have personally experienced and seen men actually speak over a woman so that her voice cannot be heard.

Perhaps being called a trailblazer is appropriate for this industry, in this city.

My career journey did not follow a well-travelled route. There were few signposts guiding my way; I often had to make my own path and determine which direction would be the best way to go. Some days, it seemed like a science experiment. I would form a hypothesis about what would be best and then try various options to test my theory and achieve a goal. Successful outcomes strengthened my theories; when the outcome was not so successful, I made adjustments and tried again.

Along the way, I learned which routes were easier to take and where there were hazards or obstacles to overcome or avoid. Through trial and error, I learned which strategies were more effective in clearing some of the hazards that blocked my path. And although it was sometimes very challenging, I realized that I was up to the challenge. We are often stronger than we think we are, and I believe that others can rise to the challenges they face too.

I think some of the wisdom I gained during my journey is unique, in that I was a visible minority female in a traditionally male profession (I was known as a landman) in a traditionally male industry. By sharing the adventures I encountered during my journey—good and bad, funny and scary—and the bits of wisdom I picked up along the way, I hope to make it easier for other women who are forging their own paths in male-dominated industries.

Over the past few years, a number of successful women have written books about the lessons they learned in the hopes of passing them along to younger women. Some of the criticism against these books is that they were written by women of privilege. I certainly don't see myself as having come from a privileged background. Both of my parents were immigrants who came to Canada in their mid-teens. I was expected to work hard at school, and as the eldest of four children, I was expected to help out in the family corner grocery store.

Ours was a fairly traditional Chinese family. My three siblings were all boys, and in the traditional Chinese culture, boys were valued more than girls. I was reminded throughout my upbringing that I was second to my brothers no matter what I accomplished. Girls were supposed to be in supportive roles; they were not supposed to take the lead. Girls were also supposed to be well behaved and quiet and were not to voice their opinions.

I was well behaved, but often not quiet. Growing up, I frequently found myself in the proverbial family shithouse for voicing an unpopular opinion. I don't blame my parents for their beliefs, as that was the way they were brought up. With limited formal education, concepts such as "equality of the sexes" were no doubt foreign to them.

There was no question that I and my brothers would attend university, and more specifically the University of Calgary, as it was too expensive to attend university in another city. We were also initially expected to choose a professional area such as medicine or law. Some may feel that the opportunity to attend university is a privilege, and I certainly can't deny that, as our parents not only pressured us, but also supported us to get a good education. However, other factors in my life contribute to my belief that I do not come from a privileged background.

Even after I was married, certain cultural norms continued to make it difficult to achieve my own goals. I chose to establish myself in my career first and delayed having a child until my early to mid-thirties. Even though the birth of my daughter brought much joy to my extended family, I again fell out of favour in the family dynamics when I decided to place my child in daycare so that I could continue with my career. My separation and divorce from my husband by the time my daughter was two added to the shame my family felt I brought onto them.

I continued to pursue my career even though I was a single mother. This was in the early 1990s, and I did not receive a lot of support from my family, as divorce was still frowned upon in the Chinese culture at that time. I needed to ensure that my daughter would grow, develop, and thrive; I also needed to focus on my career so I could provide for my daughter and make sure that she did not suffer in any way, especially economically, from my divorce. I remained a single parent all through my daughter's elementary, junior high, and high school years, as well as through her university education.

I have written this book from the perspective of someone who has not had a privileged background, but rather has persevered and forged her own path in spite of the circumstances. I will own the title of trailblazer.

However, I want this to be more than a memoir. I want to share some ideas about how I did it and the wisdom gained along the way so that this might help other women in the oil and gas industry or other male-dominated professions. The stories here may also help men to better understand what women face in their workplaces.

The first part of this book describes my background and how I entered and progressed through the oil and gas industry. The second part of the book focuses on different themes and the wisdom I gained in those areas. The themes I've chosen to write about are not an extensive set of leadership topics that are discussed in many other books. Rather, I focus on those topics in which, based on what I have learned in my own journey, women may have different approaches or experiences than men.

I hope each topic starts a conversation, even if you feel that my approach isn't directly applicable to your situation. The conversation could be between you and a mentor, coach, trusted advisor, or friend. The conversation could be among a group of women who are mentoring each other and sharing their own experiences so that others can learn from them. Sometimes it is simply valuable to know that your experience is not unique, that other women have experienced it too.

We're living in a period when women are being more vocal about their experiences in the workplace and in other arenas. The #MeToo movement is showing that women are finding the courage to speak up about situations of abuse and harassment. Perhaps this movement will also give women the courage to speak up about other situations they find themselves in where things are unfair or unbalanced.

A few years ago, someone told me that once we find our soul's purpose, things flow and become easier. After much searching, I think that my soul's purpose is to Guide, Educate, and Mentor with Grace, Integrity, and Style. I hope that you enjoy this book and that you find it helpful as you travel the path you have chosen.

THE
JOURNEY

PRE-CAREER

EVEN THOUGH I have lived most of my life in Calgary, the oil capital of Canada, I knew very, very little about the oil and gas industry while growing up in the 1960s and '70s. My family operated a corner grocery store in the Capitol Hill/ Mount Pleasant area, and we did not have any close friends or relatives working in the industry (that I can recall), so I didn't have anyone pave the way for me when I entered the sector.

When I was in grade school, my path did cross one individual who worked for an oil and gas company, though I didn't know it at the time. He and his family rented a house my parents owned in the northwest community of Charleswood for a number of years while we lived above our grocery store. I had very limited, if any, contact with him because I was so young, and it was only many years later when I was working in the oil and gas industry that I realized that the individual who had rented our house was vice president, land, of a significant-sized Canadian exploration and production company.

The first direct experience I had with an oil and gas company was when I was sixteen. I was in high school and was looking for a summer job. Given my youth and my limited skills, opportunities were scarce. This was in the early 1970s when downtown Calgary was a lot smaller than it is today, but I still had trouble navigating the maze of office buildings. I didn't even know how to read the addresses of the companies where I was trying to drop off resumés. I didn't understand that the first number was the suite number and the next set of numbers was the building address; no one had taught me that.

I finally got a job through an agency that placed temporary workers in clerical positions while employees were on vacation. I remember taking a typing test in the agency's office on a large IBM Selectric typewriter. I had never seen one before. I had taken typing in Grade 10 using a manual typewriter, so I was terrified by the electric model! Nevertheless, I did well enough on the test that the temp agency took me on their roster for the summer.

My first assignment was as vacation relief for the secretary (yes, they had secretaries in those days) for the vice president of finance of a significant Canadian oil and gas company. It was actually the same company that our renter worked for, but I didn't know that at the time.

On large eleven-by-seventeen-inch pieces of paper, I had to type the company's second-quarter financial statements using an IBM Selectric. Once I had finished the sheet and taken it out of the typewriter, I had to check it for errors. If there were any mistakes, I had to line up the sheet of paper back in the typewriter and make the corrections. I think the other secretaries felt sorry for me, as they helped me proofread the statements and tried to show me how to line up the page correctly in the typewriter to make the corrections. They told me their colleague always took her holidays when the financial statements were being prepared. I think this experience taught me to avoid the accounting area as a career—or if I ended up in this area, to be the person creating the numbers rather than the one typing up the statements.

I originally had no intention of working in an office environment. My parents immigrated to Canada in their early teens, and like most immigrants, they wanted a better life for their children. They didn't have much in the way of a formal education, and they were determined that their children would be highly educated. There wasn't any discussion about whether my siblings and I would go to university; we *had* to go, and there were some strong ideas about what we would study. One of my dad's uncles had a large family of seven boys and four girls. Of the seven boys, six of them became medical doctors. For various reasons, in our family, there was some pressure to pursue medicine as a career. From the time I started school at age five, I knew I was going to be a medical doctor—specifically, a pediatrician—and I held this belief all through high school and into my pre-med program at the University of Calgary.

Upon entering the last year of my science degree, things changed. I saw how my dad's cousins' lives were disrupted by calls during family dinners. I wanted to explore many more interests than simply medicine, but by this time, I was scheduled for interviews at two medical schools. I decided to go through with them and to attend if I was accepted. However, the passion was no longer there, and that likely came through in the interviews, because I did not get accepted.

I now had to face the question: "What do I do now?" I briefly considered becoming a lawyer, but based on what I saw on television, I decided that unless I was an exceptional lawyer, I would end up doing background work for other lawyers.

I learned that with another two years of university, I could get a business degree. That would buy me more time until I had to decide what to do with the rest of my life. So off to the Faculty of Management at the University of Calgary I went.

After my first year studying management courses, I was fortunate to land a summer position as a student placement officer with the federal government's Hire-a-Student program. The other placement officers and I took job orders from employers and helped place students in those positions. When we started in May, we were told that a number of us would be laid off in July, since the volume of jobs and students would decrease by then. We were encouraged to start watching the job boards in June to see if we could find a job for July and August.

Fortunately for me, a major Canadian oil and gas company put in an order for a mathematician. I knew nothing about the oil and gas industry (other than how to type up a financial statement from that brief summer job while in high school), but I was good at math. I applied and got the position.

The company was PanCanadian Petroleum Limited, and my position was geophysical technician supporting a consulting geophysicist. I learned a lot in two short months about the exploration side of the oil and gas industry. Near the end of the summer, PanCanadian offered to hire and train me as a junior geophysicist, because I already had a science degree. They initially said I could continue my business degree part-time and work full-time, but it was important to me to finish my business degree, so I ended up going to school full-time and working at PanCanadian part-time. At thirty-five hours per week, the job was somewhat more than part-time, but the technical training I received and the general knowledge I gained about the oil and gas industry were invaluable. I am grateful to have had this experience, as it really did set me off on my oil and gas career.

In the spring of 1979, as I was completing my Bachelor of Commerce degree, I was fortunate to have two job offers in hand. One was the junior geophysicist position at PanCanadian, and the other, which arose through campus recruiting, was for a junior landman position at Esso Resources Canada Ltd., the exploration and production arm (known as the "upstream" part of the business) of Imperial Oil Ltd. in Canada. Based on my limited exposure to the oil and gas industry to that point, I chose the junior landman position, as I believed it would be a good way to combine my interest in the technical sciences with my interest in the people side of the business. That ended up being true, and I have never regretted my decision.

OIL AND GAS
CAREER

———————————

EARLY YEARS (1979–1987)

I STARTED AS a junior landman with Esso in May 1979. While I had a general idea of what a landman did from my time at PanCanadian, I did not know the specifics of what they did or how they did it, so I had a lot to learn.

Esso had a two-year rotational training program for new landmen, with a six-month period in each of the four main areas of land: surface land, land administration, contracts, and negotiations. My specific training was adjusted slightly, as I also spent some time in natural gas marketing and hard rock minerals (such as coal), learning about what happens in those groups. This exposure to groups outside of the land department was invaluable, giving me a better appreciation of the other areas related to the exploration and production of oil and gas.

Near the end of my two-year training period, I was also nearing the completion of my Master of Business Administration degree at the University of Calgary. I was also married by this time, but we did not yet have any children, so I had the time and energy to both work and go to school. I attended classes part-time in the evenings while working full-time during the day. While this was challenging from a time-management perspective, it was great for my coursework. The MBA program included many projects, and my work gave me many real-life cases and scenarios to work on.

One such project involved the development of a new budget coordinator position to track the addition, deletion, or substitution of budget items against the total approved budget and monitor actual expenditures against budgeted amounts. When I presented the case for the new position to exploration management at Esso, they asked me if I would like to try out the role and develop it further. I readily accepted the challenge.

Taking on this role gave me the chance to better understand the full exploration process. However, it was not well received by some of the managers in the land department. In fact, one of the senior managers told me that "you were hired to be a landman, and if you don't want to be a landman, you can leave."

I was very shocked by this, because I have always believed that more information is better. If I could gain a broader view of the exploration process, wouldn't that make me a better landman? Unfortunately, this way of thinking did not fit the mould that some of the senior managers in the land department obviously wanted to put me in. Once the role was developed sufficiently, I found someone to take on the budget job permanently and I resumed my landman role.

It was probably around that time that I subconsciously decided that working in the land department of a large multinational company might not be my ultimate career path. However, I decided to try to learn as much as I could while waiting for the right opportunity elsewhere.

I learned some valuable lessons during these early days of my career. First, it was valuable to learn about the broader exploration process. I also wanted to learn about all areas of land and not be limited to one specific area.

Second, I wanted to be the one to decide which area I would pursue further, rather than have this be dictated by someone else based solely on their needs.

Third, I realized that, because I was interested in so many areas, I did not want to work for a large organization, where people were often required to be specialists. I was much more interested in being more of a generalist and learning about many parts of the exploration game.

After working at Esso for about five and a half years, I left and took on the role of land manager at a junior oil and gas company. The senior management of this company consisted of a husband-and-wife team. He was the president and she was the office manager. Those of us who worked there often wondered who really ran the company.

It became clear very quickly that the office manager wanted to exert her power over me. For example, one day she told me that I needed to limit my lunch to an hour, and that as a manager, I needed to set an example. I started to respond that I needed to build relationships with other landmen on behalf of the company and that lunches were one tool landmen used to build these relationships. However, I remembered that I did not report to her, so I told her that if the president had an issue with how I was performing my job, he should come talk to me. The president never did bring it up.

My time at this company ended when a couple of us challenged management's decision not to contribute to a retirement plan. This, of course, was at the discretion of management, but we challenged the decision because it was made retroactively after the deadline to contribute to our personal registered retirement plans, meaning we had lost the opportunity to contribute that year. We were both terminated as a result of our challenge.

This was very difficult for me, as I had never been fired from a position before. I remember going to a professional association meeting the same night I was fired, knowing that I had to network and let people know I was available. I also started calling people first thing the next morning to let them know I was looking for work. I'm proud to say that in over thirty-eight years in the oil and gas industry, that was the only day I was out of work. By the end of that day, I had secured consulting work. That was the start of my consulting company, Tiger Enterprises Ltd.

When I consulted an employment lawyer about my firing (the first time I had ever felt the need to consult a lawyer), I learned that when someone is terminated, they have an obligation to try to find work to mitigate their losses. Because I was able to mitigate my losses so quickly, there was ultimately not much of a claim.

I was with the junior oil and gas company for only a couple of years, but I did learn some valuable lessons. First, just as there are politics in a large organization, there are politics in small organizations. One difference is that you can't hide from them in a small organization.

Second, sometimes you have to find the courage to speak up and do the right thing, even though there may be some negative consequences to you personally. It is especially important to speak up if you're in a leadership position, or in situations that involve others who may be at a disadvantage or may be afraid to speak up. Integrity is key.

Third, notwithstanding the politics that can happen in a small company, I really enjoyed my experience in a smaller organization, and it helped me identify the type of company I wanted to work for.

I consulted for a few clients before joining another junior company for a short time. While there, I was exposed to various financing agreements, as one of my duties was to review all contracts that the company was proposing to sign. In addition, I learned about various software systems used to manage a company's land assets. Due to the high price of available programs, we decided to develop a simple system in-house, so I became very adept at designing, building, and populating a very large Excel spreadsheet to house our data.

MID-CAREER (1987–2000)

FOLLOWING THE SHORT tenure at this second junior company, I ended up working with a group of people for almost thirteen years in a number of companies. The first organization we worked at was sold to an intermediate-sized oil and gas company, so I learned about what was involved in a sale process. After the company was sold, I went back to consulting until the principal of this group approached me to work with him in a start-up venture.

Those were the days when you could start a company with as little as $5 million, drill a number of wells, build the company, then sell it, usually to one of the many oil and gas trust companies in existence. The same group of investors would then start a new company and repeat the cycle. It is difficult to do that these days, for a couple of reasons (besides the general state of the oil and gas industry). Many exploration wells being drilled today are pursuing what is known as unconventional resources. These are wells being drilled into shales or other source rocks at very deep levels that may require a horizontal leg or component during the drilling. These wells also often require special completion techniques before they will produce oil and gas economically. It could cost $7 to $10 million or more to drill a single well, then an additional $4 to $7 million or more to complete the well for production. In other words, you need a lot more money to start a company than in previous years.

But back in the early to mid-1990s, we repeated the cycle two or three times with the same base group of individuals. I had so much fun working in these start-up situations. Besides looking after the land needs of these companies, I often looked after setting up the office, hiring administrative staff, setting up benefits plans, and establishing other human resources functions. The times we took a company public, I worked with our advisors in reviewing offering memorandums and meeting our reporting requirements. A wide variety of tasks were involved, but they were challenging and exciting.

During this period, I learned that I really enjoyed working with small start-up companies. While access to capital is a strong reason to take a company public, there are advantages to keeping a company private, particularly if you have investors with deep pockets who appreciate the potentially longer time frame for exploration projects. I also realized that I had the capacity to learn other skills necessary to run an office.

While running a small company can take a lot of time, I valued the flexibility that these small organizations gave me. This was especially important to me in the early part of my mid-career years, as I was a new mother and newly divorced. Being a single mom puts flexibility very high on the list of things you need in a career.

After the last cycle, we essentially liquidated most of the assets of the company. Following the windup of this company, I moved the information and files on their producing assets to my home office and essentially administered their affairs for a couple of years until we were able to sell the company. I actually had our land administrator working out of my home office during this time. I remember her saying that she enjoyed coming to work in her pink fuzzy slippers but that I was pushing it when she had to deal with my sewer backup!

To keep me and my land administrator busy, it was back to finding some consulting clients. I realized that the connections I had developed over the years in the oil and gas industry were extremely important in building a thriving consulting business, which I managed to do. I also learned that the skills I had developed could be useful not only for clients such as junior oil and gas companies, but also for companies outside the traditional oil and gas industry, such as banks and the receivership arms of major accounting firms. Being creative and flexible helped me capitalize on the opportunities that were presenting themselves.

TWILIGHT (2000–2016)

N 2000, WHILE consulting for a couple of my former colleagues from Esso who had started a junior- to intermediate-sized oil and gas company, the president of this firm introduced me to two Americans who had set up a new company in Canada. In my interviews with them, they told me that our mutual contact had referred to me as a "pit bull," as I could be very tenacious. I liked what I heard about their vision for the company and I liked their energy, so I decided to join their new venture.

The new company was focused on exploring for and producing natural gas from unconventional resources—the first company in Canada to have such an exclusive intent, I believe. Their exploration focus was initially on producing natural gas from coals (sometimes referred to as coalbed methane) and then expanded to include exploring for hydrocarbons in shales. This was one of the first companies in Canada to produce coalbed methane commercially. Not only could we find it and produce it, we could make money at it!

In the sixteen-plus years I was with the company, it grew from 6 office staff to over 120 office staff plus over 20 field staff. My title changed from consulting landman to land manager to vice president of land, and we went from having a minimal land base to fairly substantive land holdings in central Alberta (primarily between Calgary and Edmonton) and northeast British Columbia.

The land base in Alberta was the result of a number of large joint ventures negotiated with some major companies in the industry. We essentially educated these companies on how to drill for and produce an unconventional resource. This was our technical advantage; we were drilling into substances that were the source rocks for the natural gas that companies were producing. In exchange, our company had the opportunity to earn an interest in the land the other companies held in the areas we explored. Each negotiation resulted in a slightly different agreement.

Our large land base in northeast British Columbia resulted from developing a detailed strategy from the onset of the project. Details such as carefully selecting the consultant who would assist us, taking the time to develop relationships with key government personnel, and developing and implementing critical land acquisition strategies all contributed to our successfully acquiring a large contiguous land base.

The strategy also depended on keeping our plans quiet within a very small team. This was difficult to do, as there were some people in our company, even within our management team, who had "loose lips." However, I knew that the strategy was working when I was sitting in an industry meeting and overheard one of our major competitors accusing another major competitor of acquiring land through a broker at a recent land sale of mineral rights. Each denied buying the rights offered up by the government, and I said nothing about our involvement.

Although our drilling results in the area showed that we could produce far more shale gas than originally expected, the remoteness of the area and the lack of infrastructure to get the gas to market made the project uneconomical.

Nevertheless, in the early days of this company, I had a lot of fun doing my part in building a large land base and putting together a group of land professionals who were excited to be working on unconventional resources. I was also involved in educating industry and government about the technical aspects of drilling and producing unconventional resources. This was particularly true in the case of joint venture partners. We educated industry landmen and lawyers about the type of agreements necessary for large, contiguous land tracts. We also educated landowners about why this was different from other resources that could be produced from their lands. Our staff and consultants needed to be educated too so that they could explain what we did to others.

This was a very exciting time in my career. Not only was I creating, building, and educating, I was learning. In order to create new clauses and agreements, I had to learn about the exploration processes focused on unconventional resources and how they differed from conventional exploration. To teach our land consultants to convey information to landowners, I first had to thoroughly understand the material myself and then had to translate the technical details into simple language so that the everyday person could understand it.

Although the company started out as a private entity, it eventually became the Canadian subsidiary of an intermediate-sized independent oil and gas producer based in Fort Worth, Texas. Unfortunately, in late 2015, the parent company entered Chapter 11 (bankruptcy) proceedings, and the Canadian subsidiary was forced to seek protection under the *Companies' Creditors Arrangement Act* (commonly referred to as the CCAA or "CC double A").

Filing under the CCAA was a condition of the sale of the company's Alberta assets. This was good for the purchaser, as they were able to secure clean title to the assets. However, it was not very good for the employees who were not offered positions by the acquiring company, did not receive any severance, and were forced to file claims as creditors through the court-appointed monitor. I was one of the employees who filed a claim as a creditor. The pool of creditors shared what remained of the company after liabilities were taken care of; creditors are often only paid pennies for each dollar they are owed, and that was the result in this situation.

POST-CAREER

AFTER BEING EMPLOYED for over thirty-eight years in the oil and gas industry (including my time at PanCanadian), I found myself unemployed in mid-May 2016. While some referred to me as being retired, I wasn't quite ready to accept that label yet, even though, financially, I could have.

At the time, I was relatively busy as a member of two boards of directors, chairing the finance committee on one board and the governance and human resources committee on the other. As I organized my post-corporate life, I tried to figure out what I wanted to do for "work." After all, one needs to work, right?

The latter part of 2016 and 2017 brought some interesting opportunities my way. Some I chose to pass on, such as developing and teaching a basic course on the exploration and production process for a company based in Iran. Others I took on, such as presenting a talk on what has changed in the upstream business in the past forty years and how this impacts the work that oil and gas lawyers do. I also taught a course in Calgary about negotiations and international contracts to two groups who worked for an oil and gas company based in Sichuan, China.

One particularly valuable contract was to do some due diligence work on properties that one company was acquiring from another. The work wasn't particularly difficult or interesting from a due diligence perspective—in fact, it was quite frustrating, because even though I could see that the selling company's files would be relatively clean from a chain-of-title perspective if they simply took one more step, they decided that they didn't want to incur the extra costs of that step. But what made this contract valuable is that it highlighted to me that this was work that I didn't want to continue to do. Sometimes knowing what you don't want to do is as valuable as knowing what you do want to do.

In 2017, as part of a concerted effort to simplify my life, I researched what happens financially when one retires from the corporate arena. There is so much to learn about during a major transition in life like this.

With respect to my board work, at the end of October 2017 I stepped down from the board of Alberta Theatre Projects, which I had been on for six years. I believe in board rejuvenation and I had completed back-to-back three-year terms, so it was time to go. Two days after my last meeting on the ATP board, I was notified that I had been appointed as a public member of the Council of the College of Physicians and Surgeons of Alberta. I also continue to serve on the board of the Calgary Convention Centre Authority.

I am now comfortable saying that I am retired from active land work in the oil and gas industry. I always keep my mind, eyes, and ears open to the opportunities that present themselves, but I have become much more discerning about what I pursue. I have my board work, I seek various speaking engagements, I am an author, I am actively involved in managing our family's rental property, and I travel.

And among all this, I have more time to reflect on my career in the oil and gas industry, and what I gained from this incredibly rewarding and sometimes challenging journey. Certain themes emerged as I thought about my experience, and the next part of the book explores these themes:

- Keep things in perspective.
- Know the numbers.
- Be creative and flexible.
- Know yourself and follow your passion.
- Be honest with yourself and others.
- Connect with others.
- Do the right thing.
- Find organizations that value diversity and your skills.
- Make decisions and live with the consequences.
- Believe in yourself.

2

GEMS OF WISDOM COLLECTED ALONG THE TRAIL

KEEP THINGS IN
PERSPECTIVE

GLITZ AND GLAMOUR

EARLY IN MY career, as part of a rotational training program, I had the opportunity to work in the natural gas marketing department of a major company. This greatly added to my experience by familiarizing me with natural gas sales contracts and Canada's pipeline infrastructure.

During my rotation through this department, I was very fortunate to work for a gentleman who had an enormous amount of knowledge in this area. Besides managing the company's natural gas agreements, he chaired both the domestic and export gas committees of the industry organization then called the Canadian Petroleum Association.

I remember the day I joined him for a meeting with a major gas purchaser. (Being the classy gentleman that he was, and still is, whenever we walked to a meeting together, he would move so that he was on the outside of the sidewalk to guard me from splashes caused by passing cars. He would do this in such a subtle way that it wasn't offensive at all. For example, the first time it happened, he basically slowed down and fell back so that he could cross behind me and reappear on my other side, closer to the street. I was talking at the time, and I didn't totally realize what had happened until I thought about it later.)

Anyway, on the day of our meeting with the gas purchaser, we finally reached the tower housing the company's opulent offices. After riding the elevator to one of the highest floors, I oohed and awed about the extensive marble in their expansive elevator lobby. But my boss made me think when he responded, "Just remember, we pay for this."

In other words, this company—known in the industry as a "cost of service" company—paid for this opulence from the fees they charged gas producers.

— WISDOM GAINED —

I LEARNED A lot about the oil and gas industry in general from this gentleman, but one of the greatest lessons was how to keep things in perspective, both in my professional career and my personal life. I try not to be swayed or impressed by the glitz and glamour I often see around me, as I consider who has paid the price for it—or if it has been paid for at all or is in fact owned by the bank.

I take a similar approach when I hear people talk about their new homes or vehicles that have the latest bells and whistles. I wonder whether they actually own their new luxury item or whether a large loan from the bank was necessary to purchase it. I would rather own my large assets outright (particularly ones that quickly depreciate in value) than be indebted to the bank.

No matter if it's glitzy offices, luxury cars, or some other shiny object, look past it for the substance underneath. Similarly, look for the substance of an individual rather than simply being blinded by their exterior facade, which can be very polished.

SENSE OF HUMOUR

EARLY IN MY career, I took things quite seriously and often had difficulty lightening up. As my career progressed, it was easier to see that some perceived obstacles were minor annoyances that would simply pass, and that it helped to have a sense of humour.

One afternoon while I was at work, I received a call from my daughter's daycare telling me that my daughter was not feeling well and that I should come pick her up. This was easy to do, since the daycare was across the street from my office. However, I needed to complete a project by the end of the week, so I brought her back to my office rather than take her home.

She really did not look well, so I decided to quickly finish my work for the day and gather up files in case I needed to work from home the next day. I kept a vinyl exercise mat under my desk for her to play on for the occasions when I had to bring her into the office. The mat had a bit of padding but it didn't have a soft cover, so I put my trench coat on it to make it a little more comfortable for her while I got organized to leave.

Shortly after my daughter lay down on the mat, I heard some gurgling noises coming from her. The next thing I knew, she threw up all over my trench coat.

After cleaning her up, I wadded the coat into a ball and put it in a plastic bag. I quickly gathered my files and we left the office. Before heading home, we dropped the plastic bag off at the dry cleaner, and I can only imagine the look on the dry cleaner's face when they opened the surprise package. I did warn them that my daughter had thrown up on the coat, but they may not have expected the large mess.

At times like this—both for me and the dry cleaner—you've got to have a sense of humour and go with the flow.

— WISDOM GAINED —

DEVELOPING A SENSE of humour can be invaluable. Whether during a particularly stressful conversation at work or when you are trying to balance the demands of work and home, finding the funny element in the situation, however small, can help ease the tension so you can get back to addressing the issues.

I am not suggesting that you find humour at the expense of another individual. Rather, the ability to laugh at something silly you have said or done can be a great strength. It makes you human and approachable. I'm not speaking about self-demeaning remarks and negative self-talk. I'm talking about observing your own behaviour in a lighthearted way and perhaps discovering other ways you could have handled a situation.

Don't take yourself so seriously, and don't beat yourself up for making a mistake. We're all human and we all make mistakes. Learn to forgive yourself as well as others. Develop a sense of humour so that you can laugh at those mistakes and move on.

KNOW THE
NUMBERS

FINANCIAL SAVVY

I HAVE ALWAYS had an interest in my personal finances. This became especially important when I became a single mom and was totally responsible for our household's financial health.

When I got divorced, I made a commitment to my daughter, even though she was only two at the time, that she would not suffer financially as a result—but with her father providing only nominal child support payments and no spousal support, since I was working, living up to this commitment required some pretty careful stewardship of the income I brought in.

Adding to the challenge was that I took on an extremely large mortgage and bank loan of almost $240,000 so I could buy my ex-husband out of his share of our family home and its contents. It used to annoy me when people would comment that I "got the house" in the divorce, when the truth was that I paid for it! Fortunately, I had good credit with the bank and a good income, so I was able to do this. But it was still a lot of money, especially when you consider that this was in 1992. I chose this path so that my daughter would not have to move out of the family home and would have some stability in her life.

I had a goal of paying down that mortgage as quickly as possible while maintaining our lifestyle. While I had assets (primarily the family home), I needed to be mindful of the monthly cash flow in and the monthly cash flow out. There was very little buffer in those early years following the divorce, but I'm proud to say that we were still able to travel extensively, and she attended top schools through her early education and university and post-graduate studies.

I know too many women who depend on their part-ners to totally handle their personal finances. When the relationships end, perhaps due to death or divorce, these competent, professional women are at a loss about what to do with their finances. I have two close friends who found themselves in this situation. One lost her husband due to his sudden death at a relatively young age, and the other lost hers in a nasty divorce. Both women came to me at various times to seek financial information or guidance or simply to bounce around ideas about their finances. They are both extremely intelligent and they quickly learned the basics and the knowledge they needed to manage their financial lives, but I think the transition was scary for them. I am so proud of them for what they accomplished in a relatively short period. As they took control of their finances, both gained confidence and become empowered.

— WISDOM GAINED —

WHETHER IN YOUR personal life or your business career, it is important to have financial literacy.

When it comes to your personal finances, remember that it's your money, and no one should care as much about this asset as you do. You need to know not only how to manage what money comes in and what goes out every month, but also how to manage your assets over the long term. This might mean working with financial advisors, and you should gain enough knowledge so that you can ask informed questions of anyone you work with. You don't have to get into all the details about how to trade shares, but you should know enough to ask the right questions about the investments your advisor might be recommending.

From a corporate point of view, you need to understand how to read financial statements so you know what they are telling you about the state of an organization. It isn't necessary to know every transaction that goes into preparing an income statement or balance sheet (unless that is your role in the organization), but you should understand the basic components of each statement and what they mean. If you did not learn about financial statements in your formal schooling, consider taking a financial literacy class.

As you move into leadership positions in an organization or onto a board, knowledge of financial statements is especially important to quickly grasp the financial health of an organization and to ask questions of the people who have prepared the statements. Keep the discussion at a higher level to identify trends. Make a point of understanding financial jargon like "EBITDA" and "ROI" so you can make meaningful contributions around the management and executive table.

Once you have a basic grasp of the financial concepts, don't be afraid to ask questions if something is unclear. If you are uncomfortable asking for clarification in a large group, find an opportunity to address your concern one on one with a trusted colleague. If you don't ask and the concept is a building block for a more complex concept, not only will you not understand the basic concept, you probably won't understand the more complex one. It is better to ask questions than to try to bluff your way through a conversation; eventually, your lack of understanding will be evident.

It's also important to understand the difference between accounting and finance. Keep an eye on the cash flow and when it comes in and goes out. Even companies with a wealth of physical assets can find themselves in difficulty if they don't have the cash to keep the lights on. These skills will be very valuable to you if you choose to move up the corporate ladder.

BE CREATIVE
AND FLEXIBLE

———————————————

CREATIVITY

_____

OFTEN, PEOPLE SAY they are not creative because they don't see themselves as an artist or a musician or an actor. If I look solely at my experience with musical instruments, for example, I would say that I'm not very creative.

I decided to take classical guitar lessons at the same time that my daughter took piano lessons. I found a talented father-daughter pair of musician-teachers so we could take our lessons at the same time. I think I had visions of being able to play like Maria in *The Sound of Music*.

After many months of lessons, my instructor convinced me to take a Royal Conservatory of Music Grade I guitar exam. So, on a hot August day, at forty years of age, I found myself sitting outside an examination room at Mount Royal University. I was so nervous and my hands were so sweaty, I wasn't sure I would be able to hold the guitar properly, never mind remember the finger positions for the notes. It only added to my nerves to look around the corridor and realize that the other candidates were eight to ten years old!

I passed the exam, even though I stopped in the middle of one of the passages and had to ask permission to start again (which I understand is unheard of). I think the examiner must have felt somewhat sorry for me. That was my first and last music exam, and I can't imagine trying to create something on the guitar.

Fortunately, there are many other ways to be creative. While working as a landman for a company on the forefront of exploring for unconventional oil and gas resources in Canada, I had to develop new clauses and agreements to deal with the exploration and production of coalbed methane. Normally, I would look for a precedent clause or agreement to work from, but there were none that applied to our situation in Canada. I had to imagine possible scenarios and try to find words to describe and make those scenarios operational.

— WISDOM GAINED —

AN INDIVIDUAL CAN be creative in many ways in a work environment. Rather than accepting that things should be done the way they always have been, consider other alternatives. If I suspect there is a better way of doing something, one of the most frustrating things for me to hear is a "because we've always done it that way" defence of the status quo. Whether that is how you structure a deal, organize a department, or resolve a conflict, look outside the normal way of doing things.

Looking at the skills you possess with a creative lens may open new opportunities for you. Breaking down the jobs you have had into the skills you have learned can help you identify other organizations who may be able to use your skills. For example, my skills include analysis (beyond land analysis), understanding finances, project management, business development, communication, mediation, and negotiations, to name only a few. Many areas in a wide range of organizations would benefit from those skills.

Some people will only see your title(s) and will not be able to look beyond your official job function. They will try to keep you in your designated box while hiring others for the new boxes they perceive they need to fill. It's up to you to convince them that you have the skills they need.

Being creative in an office environment isn't always easy. Change and the unknown often make people uncomfortable. Your creative ideas may face resistance; I certainly experienced pushback from time to time. When resistance is due to a particular reason, you may have to take small steps and develop an argument for your idea. If you make a small change and show that it benefits the parties affected, it may open the door to allow you to propose broader changes. Resistance that stems from personal or relationship issues needs to be dealt with differently, such as through mediation to resolve the problem. The key is to identify what the issue is so that it can be addressed appropriately.

Look at ways to be creative in your career and your life. Just because you don't see yourself as creative in one area doesn't mean you are not creative at all. Even though you may face resistance, looking "outside the box" allows you to explore new ways of seeing the world and possibly finding better ways to accomplish things. By looking at situations from a creative perspective, you may identify new opportunities that you have not seen before.

FLEXIBILITY

SOMETIMES WE HAVE plans for how we would like to see our career progress and how we want our lives to unfold.

After I entered the oil and gas industry, I got married and my husband and I purchased a home in the suburbs, like so many of my friends had done. I figured I would work for a number of years to establish myself in the industry before I had children. I roughly "planned" for when I would have my child(ren) within my career path. Once I had a child, I planned that I would have a live-in nanny to help me.

I did have my daughter after I had been in the oil and gas industry for about eleven years. We did have a live-in nanny for a period of time, and then we had a live-out nanny for a short while. But what I had not planned for was my discomfort with delegating "Mom" duties to a nanny. It was also difficult to adjust to having another person in the home. I also had not planned to be separated from my husband by the time my daughter was one, and divorced by the time she was two. However, being flexible allowed my daughter and me to adjust and ultimately flourish (although it didn't seem like we were flourishing on some days).

Another example of the value of flexibility came about two-thirds of the way through my career. I was very happy in my consulting firm; I had a number of good clients, I had flexibility, and I was doing well financially. But one day, the president of one of my clients stopped by my office and said he had something for me. It was the name and phone number of an individual whom my client said might have an interesting opportunity for me. "You should give him a call," he said. "They could use your help."

Even though life was running along smoothly and it wasn't necessary for me to rock the boat at that moment, I was flexible enough to follow up on that opportunity. It turned out to be an introduction to one of the principals of the company where I had the experience of being at the forefront of exploring for natural gas in coals in Canada during the last part of my career.

— WISDOM GAINED —

ALTHOUGH YOU MAY try to plan out your career and even your life, even the best-laid plans are often disrupted by unforeseen circumstances. When something unplanned happens, don't be afraid to try something new or to take a different approach.

Being flexible in both our personal and professional lives allows us to accept and adjust to the unexpected, to see and take advantage of opportunities that arise, and, ultimately, to personally grow.

RESILIENCY

THINK RESILIENCY—the toughness to bounce back from adversity—is a tremendous quality to have in life.

In the early 1990s, I certainly faced many difficulties. Granted, much was the result of my own doing, since I was the one who initiated the separation from my husband and the divorce that quickly followed.

The situation was personally stressful on many levels. My ex-husband would not leave the family home until the separation papers were signed, which was months later, and this led to a difficult home environment. I also experienced family pressures for initiating the separation and divorce. They blamed me for bringing shame to the family, so I received little support and help from them. I had a young child to look after, and I tried hard to shelter her from the nastiness in the home environment.

On a professional note, I was busy sourcing and securing consulting work, and I would often work on clients' projects after I had put my daughter to sleep. There was pressure on my cash flow as I tried to sort out how to buy my ex-husband out of his share of the family home and its contents.

The stress accumulated and there were many moments when I just needed to get through the day. Because of the dysfunctional home environment, the reduction in family support, and the need to watch our cash flow, I took my daughter to relatively low-cost venues such as the Devonian Gardens (an indoor garden) and Prince's Island Park in downtown Calgary, the public library, and the Calgary Zoo.

Through this experience, I took things day by day and I learned that I am resilient. I am strong and I have a greater capacity to deal with difficulties than I originally thought I did. I am able to look at the situation and adapt as necessary. A number of personal and professional experiences later in my life further demonstrated and reinforced that I can bounce back from adversity. I have been described as "tough" even by those who try to push me down.

From an industry perspective, oil and gas is a very resilient sector. I have seen at least three or four cycles when the commodity price drops and then rises. Each time, the industry adapts so that it can recover when prices recover. Unfortunately, the most recent cycle has been particularly long, and recovery may take longer than it has in the past and will require the industry to make major shifts.

But generally, oil and gas companies are very resilient. If oil and gas companies folded every time one drilled a dry hole (i.e., when no hydrocarbons are present), there wouldn't be an oil and gas industry. One of the reasons most companies manage a portfolio of prospects is that some of the prospects will be in areas where no hydrocarbons can be economically produced. You often do not find this out until the prospect has been drilled. Instead, these companies take what they have learned from their dry holes, adapt their models, and try again.

Most individuals who work in the oil and gas industry also have a resilient nature. They need to withstand the ups and downs of the industry but also weather the ups and downs of their respective corporate environments. Working in the oil and gas industry can be stressful, particularly because we are dealing with a commodity and have no control over its price. Factors such as global supply and demand or development of infrastructure to get a product to market are things that most of us have no control over. This creates uncertainty, and uncertainty can create stress. Individuals need to be resilient to survive the stress storm.

— WISDOM GAINED —

RESILIENCY IS A very important trait, particularly if you are in the oil and gas industry. If you don't think you naturally have it, try to cultivate it.

Think of ways to bounce back from small setbacks so you are better prepared to address larger challenges. In particularly challenging periods, remind yourself of times when you have recovered from difficulty.

Remember that, although you probably can't change the circumstances or difficulties that you face, you can always choose your attitude and the approach you take to face the challenges.

KNOW YOURSELF
AND FOLLOW
YOUR PASSION

SELF-AWARENESS

SELF-AWARENESS IS VERY important, no matter what industry you work in.

A big part of self-awareness is knowing your strengths and weaknesses (yes, we all have some weaknesses). When you know your strengths, you can find opportunities where those strengths can be best used. You can also share your strengths with others to help them develop their own. Conversely, by knowing your weaknesses, you can look for learning opportunities to reduce or minimize them. When building a team, you can look for individuals whose strengths offset your weaknesses.

Following my formal university training, for example, I knew I was good with numbers and analysis and at understanding people's psychological traits, so I did not hesitate to apply when PanCanadian Petroleum posted a job for a mathematician, even though I knew very little about the oil and gas industry. I also knew that I quickly grew bored with repetitive, mundane tasks, so when it came time in my career to build a team, I searched for individuals who loved doing that type of work so I could pursue other activities more in tune with my interests. Searching for individuals with complementary skill sets gives you a better chance of building a robust, "complete" team.

As we progress along our journey, our strengths and weaknesses will likely evolve or change. Your current strengths may get stronger and you may add new strengths as you develop your skills. New weaknesses may be identified as the environment you are in changes and you are challenged by new obstacles.

Another key part of self-awareness is knowing the kind of organizational culture that fits you best. Organizational culture can be defined as those behaviours or beliefs that govern how people behave in that organization. There are as many types of organizational cultures as there are organizations. The key is to figure out what an organization's culture is (hopefully before you join) and whether it is a fit for you.

Do you like large, formal organizations or are you more comfortable with small, more informal organizations? If you had a choice, where would you flourish?

Often, larger organizations have more formal cultures with clearly defined roles and rules. If there is a head office with regional offices, the culture within the regional offices may be more informal than the culture in head office. Geography also influences organizational culture. Companies located in Toronto or Houston tend to be more formal than many companies based in Calgary.

I recall early in my career when a senior executive visiting from head office in Toronto complained about the unprofessional way that people in the Calgary office dressed. From then on, some of my male counterparts kept a jacket and tie hanging on the back of their office door in the event of an unannounced visit from head office. Later in my career, I noticed that women working in the Fort Worth, Texas, office tended to wear nylons or pantyhose (even in the summer), whereas women in the Calgary office often had bare legs in the summer months. I remember standing in an elevator in Fort Worth with another woman, who suddenly said, "Are you wearing hose?" "No," I replied, and before I could apologize or explain myself, she said, "You're lucky; I wish I had the colouring so I didn't have to wear it."

Companies based in Asia tend to be much more formal than their counterparts in North America. North American firms looking to do business with an Asian company would be wise to research and understand the protocols and hierarchies. It is not simply knowing how to present your business card to an Asian counterpart, which is easy to learn. You need to understand the culture and the respect that is built into business dealings.

A third part of self-awareness is understanding your key drivers or motivators. Early in my career, a colleague and I were talking about various positions, and I recall the look on his face when I said, "Well, money isn't everything." After a moment of silence, he spluttered, "Well, what else is there?" As I tried to explain to him that factors like working on challenging projects, flexibility, and having a sense of accomplishment were also important, I realized we had very different motivators.

A fourth aspect of self-awareness is interpersonal relationships. Understanding how you come across to other people and your impact on them is critical to successful business relationships (there may be benefits to your other relationships as well, but my focus here is on business).

I can recall an example of a manager who was trying to be overly friendly to garner the trust of his subordinates. Unfortunately, because his approach was very forced, he came across as being fake and untrustworthy. I also remember another manager who didn't recognize that she was coming across as forceful and demanding to the point of being bullying. As a result, even though she was very intelligent, she alienated many individuals. Once that alienation happened, people tuned her out any time she spoke.

On a personal note and as an example both of different motivators and how our behaviours can be misinterpreted, someone I was dating once asked me if I disliked myself as a person. "Why would you ask such a strange question?" I responded. He observed that I was always trying to improve myself. I confirmed that I *am* always trying to improve myself because I believe that if we don't grow as an individual, we don't evolve; instead, we stagnate, and I find that to be a very sad fate. He misinterpreted my desire to improve myself as a dislike for myself as a person; I was unaware of how I came across to him. We obviously had different fundamental motivators, and needless to say, I stopped dating this individual shortly after that comment.

— WISDOM GAINED —

IT IS VALUABLE to have enough self-awareness to understand your strengths, your weaknesses, the kind of organizational culture in which you'd thrive, your unique drivers and motivators, and how you are perceived by others.

It can take a lot of internal work to identify your strengths and weaknesses. It means being brutally honest with yourself when asking questions such as, "What am I good at?" and "What am I not good at?" These questions may be harder to answer for some than for others.

If you are having difficulty identifying your strengths and weaknesses, ask a trusted friend or friends to assist you. If you are asking for honest feedback, don't be angry with those friends if they say something that you don't like. Thank them, learn from the information they provide, and adjust your behaviour accordingly.

If possible, understand the culture of the organization you work for or want to work for, and determine whether it is a good fit for you. This may be difficult to do, particularly if you are new to the industry or aren't sure what corporate culture may be a good fit for you. In this case, you just need to trust your gut or intuition when interviewing. Remember that when you are being interviewed for a position, you are also interviewing the organization.

If you are looking to do business with a company based in another city, country, and/or culture, take time to understand the cultural differences. Respect others' traditions and incorporate them into your dealings.

Be real. For example, if you are showing empathy for a co-worker's unfortunate experience, really feel empathy rather than trying to fake it. Unless you are a very good actor, people can eventually tell when your emotions are not genuine.

FOLLOW YOUR PASSION

As I WROTE in the first part of this book, I really didn't know what I wanted to do after completing my science degree. It was while subsequently studying for my business degree that I learned about line and staff positions, and I seriously considered which I would prefer.

In many industries, line positions are those involving technical skills, and staff positions are those involving people or administrative skills. I was taught that people in line positions typically make more money and move up the corporate hierarchy more quickly and to a higher level than people in staff positions. These thoughts were definitely in my mind as I considered which career path to take.

In the oil and gas industry, line positions are those that directly lead to the exploration for and production of oil and gas, such as geosciences (geology and geophysics), engineering (drilling, completions, production, and reservoir evaluation), and operations. Staff positions are typically in areas such as human resources, corporate services, accounting, information technology, and legal services.

A number of areas in the oil and gas industry blend line and staff functions. While these functions are necessary for the exploration and production of oil and gas, they may or may not involve highly technical skills, but they definitely require strong people skills. I would include areas such as land (mineral and surface), government relations, stakeholder relations, and environment and safety in this third category.

The summer before I finished my business degree was pivotal for me. I worked for two solid months in a purely human resources (staff) role at Hire-a-Student. I then worked for two solid months in a purely technical (line) role at PanCanadian Petroleum. I think those four months crystallized the staff/line dichotomy for me and made me realize I had a passion for aspects of both.

When I was later offered a junior geophysicist (line) position with PanCanadian and a junior landman position with Esso Resources, I chose land. Based on my limited experience, I believed I could combine my technical skills with my people skills. As the rest of my career would show, I was right.

— WISDOM GAINED —

WHEN CONSIDERING WHAT area of an industry to enter, don't choose something simply because you think it will lead to higher pay, advancement, or status. Rather, explore your interests and try to find a good career fit for those interests. If you don't have the skills necessary for the career that you most desire, look at ways of acquiring them. The time and energy it takes for you to acquire those skills will be well worth it if they help you get into a field you are passionate about.

While some roles remain primarily technical (line) func-tions and others remain primarily administrative (staff) functions, my experience is that many roles now require a blend of skills.

If you can find and follow your passions, going to work each day won't feel like work.

BE HONEST
WITH YOURSELF
AND OTHERS

LISTENING AND RESPECT

DURING MY CAREER, I always maintained an open-door policy where people were welcome to come in and talk about a myriad of topics. Some people felt more comfortable standing in the doorway, and some wanted to come in and sit (and sometimes close the door).

In some cases, people would stop by to ask for career advice. When the company we worked for was experiencing a period of uncertainty, I would hear questions such as, "Should I start looking for a job now or should I wait to see what happens?" In other cases, I would hear about something that was happening in another department but wasn't yet known to the executive team, such as, "A lot of people have had interviews; they're thinking of leaving the company because of how that situation was handled." Sometimes people had questions about our own department: "People are noticing that you're really cleaning out your office... is there something we should know?" If they asked a question that I was unable to answer due to confidentiality, they understood and respected that. Sometimes they needed my advice or opinion, and sometimes they just needed someone to listen to them.

I thought it was a good thing to have open communication with employees, but I once had a boss tell me that I needed to be more "managerial," as I was "too close" to the employees. After I assured him that I would never divulge any confidential information, I asked him what he meant by his comments. He said that he had observed employees coming to talk to me in my office. I told him, "I am honoured that our employees respect me and trust me enough to come speak with me."

I found out much later that a group of employees had approached him with a request to be managed by me while their manager was away on an extended sick leave. He refused and instead placed that group under another manager. Over a relatively short period, many in that group left the company, and eventually all original members of that group left. It was so unfortunate that the company lost so many talented individuals (though I am still invited to join that original group when they get together to socialize).

I suspect my boss did not approve of my open-door policy and the employees' request to be managed by me because of his own insecurities. He tried to have an open-door policy, but people who went in to speak with him reportedly spent more time listening to him talk than voicing their concerns or opinions. I believe his inability to establish open, two-way communication with his employees hampered his ability to develop trusting and respectful relationships with them (and with me).

— WISDOM GAINED —

DEVELOP TRUSTING AND respectful relationships so that an open-door policy can work. Only when there is trust and respect in a relationship can communication be at its best.

Good communication is extremely valuable not only in an office environment, but in all aspects of life. While some people are natural communicators, good communication skills can also be learned, and it is worth spending the time to practise and develop your skills. You may have tremendous ideas, but if you can't convey them clearly, whether orally or in writing, people will not hear and/or understand them.

A key element of communication is listening. And whether in a one-on-one interaction or in a group setting, you will learn more from careful, active listening with all of your senses than if you pay attention only to the words. Someone's non-verbal communication, such as their body language and tone of voice, provides additional information to the words they say. Women, mothers in particular, seem to have an uncanny ability to notice the non-verbal; develop and use that skill.

You will also gain much more information if you listen for the purpose of understanding rather than for the purpose of replying. So many people miss someone's intended message because they are figuring out how to respond to something said earlier.

HAVING DIFFICULT CONVERSATIONS

I N THE EARLY stages of the last corporate job I held, a difficult issue came up regarding two consultants who were working for me. My company had decided to rely more on employees than on consultants, since the latter were more expensive than equivalent employees, and the human resources department asked me to tell my consultants that they needed to convert to employee status. "If the consultants refuse to convert, their contracts will be terminated and we will hire employees for their positions," I was told.

I agreed to talk to the consultants, but in my initial conversations with them, I don't think I adequately conveyed the consequences of not converting to employee status. One consultant agreed to the conversion, but the other person indicated that she did not want to become an employee. She valued her flexibility and it was to her financial advantage to remain a consultant. This meant that a second, more forceful conversation was necessary.

Knowing that the consultant and I had previously worked together in other companies and that we were close personal friends, the human resources manager offered to have the second talk with the consultant. I wanted to avoid this difficult conversation, so I accepted the human resources manager's offer.

It did not go well. When the consultant held firm in her position that she did not wish to become an employee, she was terminated that very same day and was given a few hours to pack up her things.

Even though I reached out to that individual a few years later to apologize for not communicating directly with her, there were still hurt feelings. My choice to delegate the delivery of the message and avoid the necessary communication cost me a friendship.

— WISDOM GAINED —

NO ONE LIKES to have difficult conversations, but sometimes they are necessary. If you find yourself in that situation and you are the most appropriate person to have the conversation, do not delegate the task to someone else.

Learning how to structure and conduct difficult conversations can really help. For example, figure out exactly what you want to say beforehand, and focus on expressing what you see and why you see it that way, how you feel, and maybe who you are. Some useful skills include reframing, moving from "either/or" to "and" scenarios, and listening to how the other person sees the situation differently and why they see it that way.

HONESTY

W HEN JOINING A new group in the oil and gas
industry—or any industry—your reputation pre-
cedes you. Most people will give you the benefit of the
doubt to see how you perform and if you are honest and
trustworthy. Do something to break their trust, and the
story will often go company- and industry-wide.

I know of a senior executive who, after joining a
new organization that was in a joint venture with his
former company, held a town-hall-style meeting for all
employees in one of the company's small amphithe-
atres. While introducing himself to his new staff, he
significantly embellished his role in the joint venture.

A number of individuals in the audience had been
with his new company since its inception. They had
worked intimately on the joint venture project that
he spoke of. While the executive was giving his self-
introduction, many of them looked around the room
with raised eyebrows. None of them recalled him working on the project or being associated with the project.
Any credibility this individual may have had quickly
vanished, and it was difficult for him to gain trust or
respect from his subordinates from that time forward.

An issue of honesty also arose with a senior landman
I know who took on the role of land manager in a small
company. The role not only involved the technical

aspects of land work, but also needed a broad understanding of the exploration and production processes. Although this individual did not have that knowledge or experience, he believed he had the qualifications for the position and put himself forward in that light.

The job was in a junior company that needed the individual to contribute immediately, without much training time. Unfortunately, this individual was terminated within a month and has had difficulty getting a management role ever since.

While it is admirable for individuals to take on stretch assignments to further their development, people need to be honest about their capabilities not only with their employers, but with themselves.

— WISDOM GAINED —

BE HONEST, BOTH with yourself and others. Acknowledge your strengths as well as your weaknesses. Trust is such a small word, but it embodies so much. It takes a very long time to build trust. Once you have gained someone's trust, work very hard to retain it. Trust can be lost very quickly or over a single incident. People only trust leaders they respect.

Being honest about what you do not know can be difficult at times. This is particularly true when you are approached to take on a role for which you are not qualified. While this may be very good for your ego and could be a good growth opportunity, the consequences of missing key qualifications for the role could be disastrous for the company and your career.

You need to be honest with those around you in order to develop mutual respect and trust. When telling someone about your accomplishments, don't tell them you worked on a project if you didn't work on it or had only peripheral involvement. The oil and gas industry, for example, is very small, and it is easy to check out someone's story. While there are those who live by the saying "you slide farther on bullshit than brains," I believe that this will only take you so far. Dishonesty—even if you convince yourself that what you say is true—will eventually surface and will affect how you and your decisions are perceived.

CONNECT
WITH OTHERS

MENTORS AND MENTORSHIP

I NEVER HAD a formal mentorship arrangement during my time in the oil and gas industry, but I did periodically seek out and ask advice of certain individuals that crossed my path.

In the early 2000s, for example, I took coach-training courses online with an organization called Coach U out of the United States. The program recommended that we work with a coach for a while so we could experience coaching from the client's point of view.

This led me to work with an executive master coach based in the United States, and we did our coaching sessions via telephone. Each week, I had the opportunity to speak with my coach and discuss any scenarios that had come up during the week. He was not in the oil and gas industry, but that actually helped me develop my leadership skills, because it forced me to look at things from a different perspective.

During the latter part of my career, I joined a women's group organized by the Women's Executive Network. We started with eight women and a coach, who also happened to be female. The women were in a variety of industries: oil and gas, telecommunications, finance, government, and post-secondary education. While this was meant to be structured as a group coaching scenario, it evolved into a situation where the women in the group were mentoring each other. We tried to meet once a month, and at each meeting, we would try to go around the group so that everyone would have the opportunity to describe a situation they had encountered the previous month and ask advice of the group. Some months, I would have nothing significant to share, but there was value in listening to the others' stories and sharing whatever thoughts or wisdom I had about their situation. Some months, a member of the group would have a crisis situation, so the majority of the time was spent on her issue, and that was okay too. Four of us from that group still try to meet at least once a quarter to mentor each other.

While some professional organizations try to build structured mentorship programs, these programs often apply to new entrants to the industry who are in more junior positions. There are few mentors for women in supervisory or management positions who truly understand the challenges faced by a woman in the oil and gas industry. Compared to the number of men, there just aren't that many women who have reached the managerial levels—and if they have, there tends to be many demands on their time. The lack of women mentors is just one of the hurdles facing women aspiring to leadership roles.

Many of the women I know who have achieved a high level in the oil and gas industry have been helpful in promoting other women. However, I have also encountered women who have been less than helpful. I don't understand the reason for this. Perhaps they feel that since they were able to achieve their success on their own, other women should be able to do the same. Perhaps there is a jealous perception that women today have it easier than they did. Unfortunately, this sometimes results in women putting down other women for no other reason than that they are achieving a certain level of success.

— WISDOM GAINED —

MENTORSHIP RELATIONSHIPS CAN be valuable to both the mentor and mentee. To maximize the value of the relationship, goals and expectations need to be clearly set out and there needs to be a good fit between the parties.

If you can find a woman who has achieved a certain level of success in the oil and gas industry and you would like her to be your mentor, don't be afraid to ask. The worst that could happen is that she says no—and even if she does say no, she may know of someone else who has the time and energy to mentor you.

If you can't find a one-on-one mentor relationship, one alternative is to connect with a group of women who are at similar levels and are willing to meet on a regular basis to share their experiences. The women do not need to be in the same field or industry. The issues facing women in the oil and gas industry are similar to those faced by women aspiring to management roles in other sectors, particularly if management roles in those industries are predominantly held by men. It can be very helpful to share ideas and possible solutions among the members of the group.

Another alternative is to find a man who is willing to enter into a mentorship arrangement with you. However, these men may be more difficult to find. This is one of the potential downsides of the #MeToo movement. Men are being much more careful about entering into mentorship arrangements with women because they are concerned about future misperceptions that may arise.

Do your homework before approaching someone to be a mentor, whether they are a woman or a man. Have a clear idea of what you would like the relationship to be like and what the time commitment would be. Also have an idea of what you would like to accomplish while in the mentorship relationship. This will allow the potential mentor to assess whether they have the time, energy, and aptitude to assist you. Be respectful of their time, particularly if the person you approach is in a managerial or executive role.

If you are approached by a potential mentee and decide you don't have the time or energy to devote, be honest and decline. If you can connect them with another potential mentor, that could help them. Be respectful of the potential mentee. They obviously thought you had something that could assist them in their career and it took a lot of courage to approach you.

To develop your leadership skills, consider alternatives to the traditional mentor/mentee relationship, such as group coaching sessions or leadership development programs.

NETWORKING

NETWORKING IS INTERACTING with other people to exchange information and develop contacts, especially to further one's career. Networking can occur in formal and informal settings, and I've experienced the value of both many times.

Early in my career, for example, I volunteered for the education committee of the Canadian Association of Petroleum Landmen (CAPL). I realized very quickly that senior landmen or land executives in the industry would take or return my calls because they weren't sure if I was calling about a CAPL matter or a company matter.

Another networking activity I participated in early on was to attend many of the formal networking programs established strictly for women—though I remember being very disappointed. Essentially these were groups of women standing around handing out business cards. The gatherings almost felt like competitions to see who could hand out and collect the most cards. Fortunately, women's networking events have improved over time. Often there is an educational component (a talk or a panel discussion) along with time for networking. Often men are in attendance, but the vast majority of attendees at these events are women. My observation is that women have learned how to network while incorporating some of their social skills.

While many people consider networking to be formalized activities like these, I learned that my informal networks could do as much if not more for my career. During my mid-career years in the oil and gas industry, I curled competitively and was an instructor in the Southern Alberta Curling Association's (SACA's) "Learn to Curl" program. One of the main volunteers at SACA happened to be an engineer in a junior oil and gas company.

I had not had any professional contact with his company to that point in time, but one day this engineer called me at the office to ask if I was free for lunch. When I said yes, I found out that I wouldn't be having lunch with my curling colleague. Instead, he suggested that I meet his company's president. I went to lunch, met a very nice man who also happened to be a curler, and had a very pleasant conversation about a variety of topics.

"What is your favourite position on a curling team?" he asked me at one point during the meal.

"I like the third position because I like being involved with the strategy and I like the physical exercise of sweeping," I said. "This all assumes I am playing for a skip I have confidence in. Otherwise, I would play the skip position."

I guess he must have liked my answer, because at the end of the lunch, he said, "What would it take to make you leave your current position and cross the street, and when could you start?"

This took me by complete surprise, and I told him I would get back to him. After returning to my office and doing some salary research, I quickly got back to him with the information he requested, and I ultimately accepted the position. Informal networking got me started with a group that I had a lot of fun working with throughout the middle years of my career.

— WISDOM GAINED —

THERE ARE MANY opportunities to network—some informal, and some formal. Informal networking is what happens during gatherings with family and friends, for example. Sometimes at these gatherings there is an opportunity to meet someone new, who may or may not be in your industry. Sometimes it's simply having the time to interact with someone in a totally different way. For example, who knew that in speaking with that second cousin at a family wedding reception you'd hear that they are now employed at an entry level in your industry? Or that the individual you've just met at a large banquet went to the same high school as you and that you had the same teachers?

If you have children, their participation in sports can offer another informal setting for networking. Meeting and learning something about the other participants can lead to opportunities to connect outside of the playing field or sports arena.

Formal networking settings include the regular lunches or breakfasts that many professional associations host for their members. Make an effort to attend these, and instead of always sitting with your friends or individuals you already know, introduce yourself to someone new. Another excellent way to expand your network is to volunteer for a committee of your professional association.

As you practise networking, your range of contacts will greatly expand. You may find that you have contacts from your career, from your extracurricular activities, from your family, from your past schooling, from your children's school, and so on. This is all okay. But networking is not just about building your contacts list or increasing the number of connections you have on LinkedIn. It is all about developing relationships.

The next time you're at a gathering of any sort, reach out to an individual you don't know or don't know well, even if you are very shy. Be curious about them and explore what is important to them. Be willing to share a bit about yourself. Sometimes it is scary to take that first step, but over time it does get easier and you will expand your life experience through the people you meet.

And remember that networks flow both ways. Just as you can be assisted by someone, you may find yourself in a position to assist others.

GIVING BACK

I AM EXTREMELY grateful to have had the opportunity to work in the oil and gas industry. It has been an interesting journey with many challenges, but also many rewards. One way I have shown my appreciation is by giving back to the industry and my community.

Though I have given back in a number of ways throughout my career—and still do—helping to establish the Petroleum Land Management concentration in the Bachelor of Commerce degree program at the University of Calgary is one of the accomplishments I am most proud of.

In the early 1980s, the only formal university education path for a student wanting to pursue a career as a petroleum landman was to go to the United States. Mount Royal College (now University) offered a two-year program, but students had to transfer to a university in the United States to finish their degree.

Board members of the Canadian Association of Petroleum Landmen decided that it would be beneficial for the industry and potential students to have a program at the University of Calgary. The original, simplistic vision was for the University of Calgary to train negotiating petroleum landmen, Mount Royal College to train contracts landmen, the Southern Alberta Institute of Technology to train land administrators, and Olds College to train surface landmen.

The dean of the University of Calgary's Faculty of Management struck an ad hoc committee to investigate the proposal. On the committee were a senior landman from a major oil and gas company, a senior professor from the University of Calgary, and me. While the senior landman focused on securing funding for the program, I worked extensively with the professor to develop the program details, including required courses and course outlines. I remember sitting on my porch, overlooking an expansive view of downtown Calgary, in the summer of 1982 with a stack of proposed course outlines needing review and refinement.

The program was structured so that core courses in Petroleum Land Management would be taken in the final two years of the Bachelor of Commerce program. Successful graduates would be granted a Bachelor of Commerce with a concentration in Petroleum Land Management. The final proposal went before the Faculty of Management in June 1983. The program was eventually approved, funds were raised during 1984, and classes in the program started in the fall of 1985.

Through 2017, the program has given 511 graduates a good start in the oil and gas industry. The program is currently being re-examined, with thoughts of expanding it to a broader energy focus.

— WISDOM GAINED —

THERE ARE MANY ways to give back. It could be through sharing your time, money, or expertise, or any combination of these. You may also find other creative ways to contribute to your profession, your industry, your community, or society as a whole, and it can be at whatever level you determine works best for you.

Early in your career, you may not have much time to give back to the larger community, particularly if you have small children and are involved in their activities. As you progress in your career, you may find that you are in a better position to volunteer or give back in other ways.

Sometimes the volunteer activities you perform will directly impact your career due to the people you meet. However, that is not the primary reason to volunteer. Giving back allows you to go beyond what you as an individual can accomplish in your lifetime. It never ceases to amaze me when I hear how one small comment I have made or a small action I have taken has impacted the lives of others.

DO THE RIGHT THING

—————————————

COURAGE

LATE IN MY career, I worked on a major project with another company vice president and a consultant whom he brought in for the project ("his" consultant, he liked to say).

I had just returned to the office following the September Labour Day holiday after taking a couple of weeks of summer vacation. I met with this vice president and the consultant for an update and to prepare for a meeting later that day with a senior manager of an overseas company that was considering a joint venture with us for the project.

The overseas company had sent over a young engineer early to do some due diligence and analysis, and my colleagues had met with him in my absence. As they updated me, they told me they had taken the engineer to a local strip club one evening. They laughed about how uncomfortable he had appeared, and that his "eyes were *this* big." They also laughed about how the strippers had preferred their company to that of their younger, Asian counterpart.

"The next time we go," they said to me, "you should come with us, because there were women in the club."

"Some of these women don't have a choice about the type of jobs they take," I responded. They were quick to point out that there were women in the audience and repeated that I should go with them next time. I quickly left the office, saying that I had to get ready for another meeting.

This was not the first time I had experienced these types of comments from these two individuals. We had travelled internationally together, and one night while sitting in the lobby bar of a high-end international hotel to debrief the day's activities, I had been shocked when they loudly said, "Oh my gawwwd," as a beautiful woman passed by. They made similarly loud, juvenile comments as other beautiful women went by our table. It was embarrassing and offensive, and I finally excused myself for the evening when the behaviour continued.

The evening after I learned about their strip club shenanigans in Calgary, the three of us had dinner at a Chinese restaurant with a senior manager from the potential joint venture partner. I was dismayed when they started to tell him that they had taken his young engineer to a strip club. Their story was interrupted by a waiter who asked whether they wanted rice with their dinner. They said they wanted sticky rice, then looked at each other and burst out laughing. "I wonder what makes it sticky," one said. They were laughing so hard at their "joke" that they couldn't even talk. I certainly wasn't going to explain to our guest what they were laughing at! He simply looked at me, shrugged his shoulders, and said, "They are just like children."

What a way to impress a potential partner!

Even though I had seen the vice president and his consultant engage in crass and unprofessional behaviour multiple times, I hesitated to bring this forward to my boss—who was also the other vice president's boss. I worried about retaliation, my reputation, and whether speaking up would make any difference.

Later that week, however, at an industry golf tournament, I was playing in a foursome that included three other female senior landmen. When I relayed the story and asked for their advice about whether I should speak up, their initial reaction was shock that this behaviour would happen in this day and age. When I pressed my cart mate for her opinion, she said, "You have to speak up, because you are in a position to do so." What she meant was that if this had happened to a younger person, such as a junior technologist or a junior support staff individual, they would be too afraid to speak up and things would not change.

Back at the office, I prepared notes describing the behaviours, then asked my boss for a meeting. "I'd like to discuss a situation that you should be aware of," I said. I nervously sat down in his office with my notes in hand and described the behaviours. My boss's initial reaction was disappointing and discouraging. He laughed and said something to the effect of "boys will be boys."

I knew that he had a young daughter studying business in university, so I asked him, "How would your daughter feel if she was subjected to this type of behaviour? How would *you* feel if she was?" It was only then that he took me somewhat seriously. "What would it take to make this go away?" he asked. I wasn't expecting the question, so I said I would think about it and get back to him.

After mulling it over for a couple of days, I asked my boss to request a written apology from the other vice president. I also suggested that I be taken off the major project we'd been working on together. My boss was surprised at this second request, as it was a significant project for the company. "Don't you want to work on this project?" he asked.

"Of course I do," I replied. "It's not often in your career you get an opportunity to work on a project from geological conception to export out of Canada." Even so, I said that it was probably better for the project if I was taken off the team. What I didn't share with him was that I could see from recent meetings that my contributions to the project were being minimized, even though I was of Asian heritage and I understood the culture of the potential joint venture partners. I also did not think we would ever be able to achieve an agreement with this company or any other company. (It would turn out that I was right about this last point. Even though many resources continued to be devoted to this project, no agreement was ever achieved with this or any other firm.)

I don't know what my boss told our head office or our potential joint venture partner about my departure from the project, but by stepping away from it, I knew I would not have to continue to deal with this juvenile behaviour.

Many months later, as the company was in the final stages of divesting our Canadian assets, I was sitting in my office one afternoon surrounded by conveyance documents when I received a phone call from our head office general counsel, who was also our chief compliance officer. After the normal civilities, she told me she had just heard of the incident I had reported to my boss several months earlier. "Why didn't you bring any of this to my attention?" she asked.

I explained that I had taken it up the chain of command and, quite frankly, was concerned about retaliation. "Well, we take this very seriously, and I wish you had brought it up at the time it happened," she said.

So you see, it's not only junior staff who are concerned about the ramifications of speaking up about issues like this. Sharing stories of incidents like this can be embarrassing, and there is often a fear of reprisal, no matter if you are the victim or a third party who has witnessed the behaviour. Often, these reprisals are informal and can be very subtle. For example, after speaking out about the incident described above, I found out that I was being excluded from executive meetings. When I questioned my boss about this, he said that he forgot to invite me or that he didn't think I would be interested in the topic. I started to pass by meeting rooms when I thought a meeting was taking place that I should be attending.

I'd just like to make a side comment on leadership. If a senior executive or manager is a bully, the people who work for them will see that this type of behaviour is acceptable in the organization and may also start to exhibit bullying behaviour, as it all flows down from the top. Even though my boss didn't engage in the objectionable behaviour, he perpetuated it by turning a blind eye to it. A failure in leadership in this area can create a truly toxic environment.

This is not the only time I experienced or heard about harassing or bullying behaviour in the oil and gas industry—unfortunately, there are all too many stories I could share here. But the longer I have been in the industry and the older I get, the more willing I am to speak up when I see something that is not right. Perhaps it's because I have found my voice or perhaps it's because I am not as concerned about the ramifications. Whatever the reason, I have found my courage.

— WISDOM GAINED —

THE BOTTOM LINE is that no one deserves to be the target of harassing or bullying behaviour. If you see or experience behaviour that is wrong, have the courage to speak up. I know this is difficult, particularly if you are young or new to the industry or company. It's even difficult when you are a seasoned veteran in the industry. If we want things to change and we expect things to improve, it's essential that we all take a stand.

There is no one right way to deal with unprofessional behaviour. You have to take into account the situation, the individuals involved, your relationship with those individuals, and the consequences of any action you may take. Sometimes a bit of trial and error is required to see what will work in a particular situation or corporate culture.

Pick your battles so that you speak up for principles that are really important to you or that have the potential to impact others. To deal with any fears you may have, ask yourself what is the worst thing that could happen if you speak up. Then ask yourself if you can deal with that.

If you don't think you can deal with the consequences, are there other actions you can take? Perhaps you can choose one of the other strategies and live to fight another day.

It is important to actively choose a strategy, even if that strategy is "do nothing . . . for now." Understand that doing nothing may have consequences of its own, such as internal conflict resulting from not speaking up when you know it is the right thing to do.

If you can deal with the consequences, speak up. Rather than verbally attack the harasser or bully, tell them that you view their behaviour as inappropriate and that it is making you uncomfortable—no one can dispute how you feel. A pointed comment can also sometimes get through to the individual, and occasionally, other people may be present who can assist by chastising the individual or removing him from the situation. Unfortunately, this won't necessarily change the behaviour for the next time, particularly if the individual is intoxicated.

If you're not having any luck dealing with the individual directly and the offensive behaviour continues, have the courage to bring your concerns up a level, either to the individual's supervisor or manager, the human resources department, or the company whistleblower, if there is one. Depending on your organization's culture, you may unfortunately get the response that I did a number of times, and that was that "boys will be boys." When I heard that, I always wondered when these so-called boys would be expected to behave like professional men.

I have heard some men comment about having to be careful in the #MeToo era. Some have suggested (jokingly, I hope) that perhaps women shouldn't be in the workplace so there is no temptation. From a woman's perspective, that is definitely the wrong focus. The focus should be on addressing men's unacceptable behaviour.

Individuals have been reluctant to come forward about harassment, bullying, or other unprofessional behaviour in the past, particularly in leaner economic times when layoffs were common and jobs were scarce. Perhaps the #MeToo movement will encourage people to come forward more often and in real time.

INTEGRITY

_____

EARLY IN MY career, as a woman aspiring to a management role in the technical side of the oil and gas industry, I felt I sometimes had to walk a very fine line. I wanted to be a part of the team, so I went along with some of the shenanigans that went on. Sometimes I and other women were simply excluded from activities, but other times there was pressure to participate with the men in certain goings-on, and it took courage to maintain my integrity and insist that others maintain theirs.

During a golf tournament in the early 2000s, I witnessed something that showed how little this reality had changed for younger women just entering the industry. It was a very hot, sunny day in August in Canmore, Alberta, and this was a tournament known for the amount of drinking on the course. (I once asked the general manager of the golf course why they tolerated this, and he admitted it was their highest-grossing event.)

Given the amount of alcohol consumed, some crazy shenanigans were always inevitable. Even so, imagine my surprise when I saw two golf carts come around the corner carrying three men who were all down to their boxer shorts, and one young woman down to her bra and panties.

The men were all experienced industry veterans, and the woman was a recent graduate. There was a huge power imbalance between them, and I have no doubt that the young woman was a victim of peer pressure. Still, I wanted to go up to her, shake her, and tell her that this was not the way to make her mark in the industry if she wanted to be taken seriously. I also wanted to tell the men that their behaviour was highly inappropriate... but I didn't. At that point in my career, I still tended to joke away inappropriate behaviour like this, or I tried to ignore it. Only toward the end of my career did I become much more vocal about addressing it directly.

You would think that professionals in the oil and gas industry—in any industry—would behave in a professional manner. Unfortunately, that is not always the case, and that is very sad, both for the individuals and for the companies they work for. I once thought it was just the senior members of the industry that sometimes behaved this way, and I had hoped that younger generations would be more enlightened and aware of their behaviour and the impact on their professional relationships. Unfortunately, that does not appear to be the case.

— WISDOM GAINED —

THEY SAY THERE are six degrees of separation—that is, everyone is only six or fewer relationships away from everyone else. I believe that in the oil and gas industry in Calgary, it is more like two degrees of separation. The power of networking is strong. Therefore, be aware that other people in your network will likely find out about your actions even if they have not directly observed them.

No matter what industry you work in, your reputation is one of the most important things you can protect. Reputation is based on behaviour, and no matter how you were brought up, you can choose to behave with integrity—that is, with an adherence to moral and ethical principles.

It takes courage to maintain your integrity when everyone around you is taking the low road. It takes courage to stand your ground when others are trying to convince you to take another, less desirable route. And it takes courage to insist that others behave with integrity too.

FIND
ORGANIZATIONS
THAT VALUE
DIVERSITY AND
YOUR SKILLS

———————————

DIVERSITY

IN THE EARLY years of my career, I did a lot of volunteer work for my professional association. After serving on the education committee for a few years, I was elected as a director of the association, and I served a couple of one-year terms. Evidently, however, I was oblivious to the politics that were happening behind the scenes.

The morning after I lost an election to serve for a third term, I received a call from a friend who was acting as my pseudo–campaign manager. "I think it is awful what some members did," he said. I had no idea what he was talking about, so I asked him to explain.

"A group of men called members in their network telling them not to vote for the women on the ballot," he replied. "The men said that in these tough times, women are taking away jobs that rightfully belong to the men." This was in the mid-1980s, and I was speechless.

That experience led to my doing very little volunteer work for my professional association until much later in my career, when I was once again elected as a director, this time for a two-year term. However, I ended up being the subject of further political manoeuvres when I tried to run for an executive position in the late 2000s. All of a sudden, a couple of my supporters on the board who were unable to attend a critical meeting were not allowed to vote in absentia either by phone or by proxy, even though such votes had previously been allowed by the board. It appeared that not much had changed in the twenty-plus years that had passed since I had first experienced political shenanigans. I did not volunteer any further time or energy to that organization.

Unfortunately, this wasn't the only time I bumped up against such bias. When I started my board education with the goal of eventually joining a board, I was actually told that I wouldn't get a board position in Calgary unless I was male, white, and old. I responded that I was coming up on the "old" piece, but that I didn't have a chance with the other two criteria. Although this may have been said somewhat in jest, there was definitely some truth in it.

When I first encountered such bias against women in the oil and gas industry, I wasn't quite sure how to deal with it. Fighting against it was often ineffective and simply provided more ammunition for men to justify why they should hire or promote other men over women.

I was also leery of anything that smacked of reverse discrimination or tokenism—any programs that sought out the underrepresented sectors to add to a team with the specific purpose of increasing diversity. I felt that you should search out the individual whose skills and experience are the best fit for the position, regardless of gender or ethnicity.

An individual I once worked for told me that if he had an opportunity to hire a man or a woman who had identical education and experience and were at the same level in the industry, he would always hire the woman. I initially felt indignant at this remark until he added that he would hire the woman because she would have had to work harder to get to the same level and she should be recognized for that. That's a very interesting observation, but likely very true. I wish others had the same insight.

I still maintain the basic position that the best person should be hired for the job, male or female, but in my later years I started to understand why some women view diversity programs as a way of getting their proverbial foot in the door. Once in, after a woman proves (many times) that she actually has some skills to contribute, she will hopefully be given the opportunity to add value.

Similarly, when I first heard that some countries have adopted a quota system to require publicly traded companies to have a certain percentage of women on their boards, I wasn't sure I was supportive of the idea. But with so little progress in increasing the percentage of women on for-profit boards in Canada, I'm wondering if having quotas is the only way to make a significant shift in the numbers.

There may be a backlash against women as an unintended consequence of the movement to increase diversity on boards. I have heard older, white men blame the current focus on increasing board diversity for their inability to get on boards and that women have an advantage over them. While there may be some truth to this, the number of available board positions has also decreased compared to the number of people striving to get a paid board position.

As for my own board endeavours, I finally adopted the attitude that certain individuals and companies would not change, and that it was their problem that they were missing out on over half the talent out there. I chose to devote my board energies to organizations that do value and practise putting diversity into action more than the oil and gas industry does, yet can still use the skills that I bring from this industry. I served for six years on a theatre company board and am currently serving on two government boards (one municipal and one provincial).

— WISDOM GAINED —

YOU ARE NOT going to change the behaviour of those who don't really value diversity, even if they preach it. You can't fight every battle, so instead of wasting a lot of time knocking on and trying to get through doors to organizations that don't put a priority on diversity, search out more enlightened individuals and organizations that value you and the skills you can bring to the table.

While there is still a diversity gap in the for-profit world, there is something to be said for helping a not-for-profit organization achieve its goals. Often there is no monetary compensation, but the intangible "feel good" rewards of doing good for an organization or your community will make your efforts worth it.

BRING YOUR POWER

WHEN I STARTED my career, popular books such as *The Woman's Dress for Success Book* described the female equivalent of the power suit. The message was that if we wanted to be successful, we needed to wear clothes that emulated what successful males wore. My wardrobe reflected what I read in these books: black, navy, and grey suits with the required big shoulder pads, white blouse, and coordinating silk scarf. While conservative dress is important if women want to be taken seriously in the oil and gas industry, thank goodness we no longer have to copy men's outfits to be effective.

This apparent requirement to copy men showed up in another form in the corporate world, as I soon discovered. Within the first five years of my career, I was given the opportunity to take some psychological tests that my company used to predict the suitability of an individual for management positions. After taking the tests, I met with the company psychologist to review my results.

In our meeting, the psychologist asked if I had any questions. I did! "How were the questions developed?" I asked.

"Why do you want to know that?" he responded.

"Well," I explained, "I felt that the questions were biased in favour of males. They were looking for typically male traits." Although I do not recall the exact wording, there were questions such as this:

In high school, I participated in the following sports:

☐ football
☐ basketball
☐ tennis
☐ gymnastics
☐ badminton

In high school, I participated in the following activities:

☐ student government
☐ debate club
☐ art club
☐ chess club
☐ yearbook club

While I was growing up, my mother was:

☐ in the Women's League
☐ part of the women's group at the church
☐ a member of the sewing circle
☐ a member of a book club
☐ a businesswoman

The questions clearly favoured males, as they were looking for traits such as working on teams and leadership qualities. Fortunately for me, I played a number of team sports in high school and sat on our student council for two years, first as secretary and then as president. My mother ran a corner grocery store, so I saw her as a businesswoman. (I didn't even know what the

Women's League was.) The questions also likely had an Anglo-Saxon bias, but I didn't focus on that, since the male bias was so obvious.

The psychologist indicated that they looked at the traits and background of the senior leadership of the company and then formulated their questions to draw out these characteristics. I then asked, "How many females are there in the senior leadership team?" I don't think he was too impressed with my question. As I recall, there were very few, if any, females in this elite group.

I also vividly remember the psychologist saying that his concern with most female employees was that they would not be able to have the difficult conversation involved in terminating someone. "But my concern with you," he said, "is that given the appropriate information and circumstances, you would have no problem terminating the individual."

The psychologist's view was all too common. Assertive women were called "aggressive" or "bitches" (or worse), while the same behaviour in men was referred to as "decisive." While men were allowed to curse and act tough, women were expected to be quiet and compliant. Men could drink and often be loud and belligerent, but it wasn't ladylike for a woman to do so.

Sometimes, successful women were simply referred to as "one of the guys." This happened to me more than once. In the middle of my career, for example, the company I worked for organized a field trip for one of our board members following a board meeting. Our president (who was a geologist), our engineer, and I were going to show the board member some of our wells in southern Alberta, which we could drive to on a day trip.

To make the most effective use of our time, we decided that we would prepare lunch on the road. I recall someone had rented or borrowed a large motorhome, and I was assigned the task of picking up sandwich fixings.

When we went to pick up the board member from his hotel, our former chief financial officer (who now worked for the chairman of the board) came out to see the motorhome. He stepped in and said, "Wow, where are the dancing girls?" I was standing right there, so I looked at him, raised my hands palms up, and said, "Ahhh?"

He just shrugged it off and said, "I don't see you as a girl; I see you as one of the guys."

"Thanks, I think," I said. (Interestingly, he told me much later, "I hope that my daughters can achieve as much as you have.")

Over time and through experimenting in many situations, I realized that I could be "just one of the guys" when I needed to be, but that in the appropriate circumstances, I could bring some unique strengths as a woman to a team, such as empathy and compassion in an emotionally charged situation, or collaborative mediation skills to defuse a potentially explosive meeting. I learned to embrace these skills as part of my tool box— or should I say, "jewelry box." The techniques that I employ, whether characteristically masculine or feminine, depend on the situation at hand.

— WISDOM GAINED —

THE OIL AND gas industry is still very male-dominated, with misogyny practised in many thinly veiled ways— whether it's taking a woman's childrearing responsibilities into account when considering whether to promote her into a senior position, excluding women from corporate outings involving senior executives and board members, making sexual comments or jokes, or excluding women from boardrooms.

We need to call out these attitudes and practices and bring them out into the open so they can be discussed. We also need to acknowledge that women should not have to manage like men to be successful as leaders. Many of the skills that women practise on a daily basis, such as emotional intelligence, empathy, collaboration, motivating others, diplomacy, and time management, are now being recognized as valuable leadership skills.

Take negotiations, for instance, which have been a large part of my career. The approach to negotiations has evolved significantly from when I started my career to the present, shifting from a win-lose approach to a more collaborative win-win approach—an approach that women are especially well suited to. Through our lives outside of work, we already understand the importance of relationships and have frequently needed to collaborate with others to accomplish goals in our lives.

Women leaders do manage differently than men, and that is okay. One is not necessarily better than the other; they are just different. A woman's style may be more appropriate in certain situations, and a man's approach may work better in other situations. Learn which skills are important and most appropriate to apply to the situation at hand.

MAKE DECISIONS
AND LIVE WITH THE
CONSEQUENCES

——————————————————

CHOICES

I HAVE ALWAYS believed that it is good to have choices in life. I much prefer having choices than being in a situation where there isn't one.

Still, choices can be tough to deal with! I was a vice president and about twenty-one years into my oil and gas career when I had to make one of the toughest choices I've ever faced.

It began with a phone call from a colleague who was starting a new junior oil and gas company with a group of investors. It was a bright, sunny day outside, but I was immersed in files in my home office as he started to tell me about his new venture.

I assumed he had called to talk about a land deal, but then he cut to the chase: "We want you to join us as president of the new company," he said.

My jaw dropped, and at first I was speechless! Those who know me well will attest that I am not often speechless. What an opportunity! The job came with a higher salary than what I was then making as a consultant, the chance to grow a company from its beginnings, and the prestige of being a woman president of a junior oil and gas company.

However, there were also some pretty steep personal costs to consider: building a start-up company from scratch would take a lot of time and energy. As a single mother, I thought that my preteen daughter would need more "Mom" time in the coming years and that I would need to be more available for her. If I took the position that was offered, I would have to spend a lot of time growing this new "baby," and I worried that my relationship with my daughter would suffer.

I promised my colleague I would think about it, and then I did what I always do when I have to make a major decision. I gathered more information and, over the next few days, played out the scenarios of each option: "If I choose this option, this may happen; if I choose this other option, this may happen." As it almost always is, one of my options was to do nothing. I analyzed that scenario as thoroughly as I did the idea of becoming the new company's president.

As I considered the pros and cons of each option, one of the questions I asked myself was "What would I do if I were not afraid?" I thought about what scared me about the hypothetical outcomes of each choice and if there was anything I could do to reduce or remove those fears. This way of looking at choices, which I discovered fairly late in my career, can make options less overwhelming to consider, or can even introduce new choices.

After weighing everything in my analysis, I was able to make a conscious decision. The personal costs of taking on this new opportunity outweighed the pros, so I declined the offer. I have never regretted my decision, as I continued to nurture and help develop my original "baby," resulting in a very strong relationship with my daughter. At least I had a choice.

— WISDOM GAINED —

CHOICES ARE ACTUALLY opportunities. No matter what situation you find yourself in, when you have a choice, you actually have an opportunity to influence what happens next, rather than just letting things happen to you.

When you make a decision, make sure it is an informed one. Do your research, analyze the information, understand the consequences of each option, and be prepared to live with those consequences, positive and negative. Remember that one option may be to do nothing. Deciding to do nothing is still a conscious choice.

Asking "What would I do if I were not afraid?" can be a very useful way of exploring your options further.

LIFE-WORK HARMONY

I LIKE THE phrase "life-work harmony" better than "life-work balance," because the word "balance" suggests that it is a 50:50 ratio, and that isn't always the case throughout your career. Sometimes work takes on a more important role, and sometimes life requires more of your time and energy.

When I started in the oil and gas industry in the late 1970s, there was a myth that the superwoman could do it all: be a loving, supportive, and sexy spouse, a great mother, and a successful businesswoman, all while keeping herself healthy and active. Based on my experience, there isn't time to accomplish all of this, so I believe that one has to establish priorities, make choices, and delegate some tasks. I also know that, no matter how much "planning" you try to do, life always manages to throw some curveballs, and you just have to deal with them.

Maintaining harmony between life and work was very important to me throughout my career, but particularly after I became a mother. When my daughter was born, I had been in the oil and gas industry for just over eleven years and was working as a consulting landman. There were still two weeks to go in my pregnancy when I went in for a procedure one Friday to "turn" the baby, as she was sitting horizontally across my uterus.

For safety reasons for the baby, it was decided that day that I should have a caesarean.

My main client at the time was a major oil and gas firm, and I remember calling the individual supervising my work at the client's office the following Monday to tell them I wouldn't be in that morning because I was in the hospital with my baby.

My baby was slightly jaundiced, and I remember the doctor saying, "You could go home now, but if she needs to come back for treatment, she'll be put in peds [the pediatric ward], and I don't want her there." As a result, I stayed in the hospital for a week until she was ready to go. I vividly remember signalling a nurse to come back when she came to take my vitals, as I was on a telephone call with another client to talk through an agreement I was drafting for them. She left the room shaking her head.

Initially after the birth, I worked out of my home office. Being a working mom, I needed help with childcare, as my husband did not help out much with household and childrearing duties. We tried a live-in nanny for a while, then a live-out nanny, until deciding to place our daughter in a daycare centre. Her father supported the idea, as he liked the income I was able to bring in, but I did not receive any emotional support from my immediate family for this move, even though it was an exceptional childcare centre. Prior genera- tions "did not put their children in daycare," they said. They were especially critical that I was working out of my home office for the first year or so that she was in daycare. Our families couldn't understand why I couldn't just keep her at home while I worked.

Partially because of this family pressure, I felt so much guilt about leaving my daughter that first day I took her to daycare. The childcare centre was on the third floor of an office tower on the west side of downtown Calgary, and it was clean and bright and had lots of colourful toys for the children to play with. When I handed my daughter over to the daycare worker, she promptly began crying and screaming. I went out of that room and around the corner, and I stood there for quite a few minutes with tears streaming down my face. When I heard my daughter stop screaming, I peeked around the corner and could see that the childcare workers had distracted her with a toy and other activities. I stayed until I could see she was okay. The staff assured me she would be fine, and she was.

By the time my daughter was one, I was separated from my husband after eleven years of marriage. By the time she was two, I was divorced and a single parent. I was working out of an office tower in the central downtown core by then, and I was able to move her to another highly regarded daycare in an office tower across the street, which made it convenient for me to visit her during lunch hours. She still remembers walking through downtown Calgary's elevated indoor walking system to a food court, where we would often share a Wendy's frosty.

I am so grateful for the staff of those exceptional childcare centres, as they allowed me to continue building my career. More importantly, they helped my daughter develop essential social skills at an early age. Many, many years later when my daughter was in university, she thanked me for putting her in daycare. She said she learned how to interact with others and to share. I was very grateful for her comment, as I still carried some guilt about putting her in daycare, since both of her cousins on my side of the family had stay-at-home moms. I was finally able to release that guilt.

From the moment I became a mother, my first priority was my daughter, both her well-being and her development. My physical and mental well-being was lower on the priority list, but I understood that if I didn't look after myself, there wouldn't be anyone to look after my daughter. Other items such as having a pristine, orderly house or being employed in a high-power position were much, much lower on the priority list. I had to give up the idea that I would be the perfect supermom and career woman. I had already given up the idea of being the perfect spouse. Some days, I just needed the strength to get through the day.

Over the course of my career, I have attended presentations by women who have achieved much in the oil and gas industry. Often these presentations were on how they had achieved their success and how others could do it too. Besides working hard in their chosen field, they often had a supportive spouse and no children, and I remember thinking that their situations were vastly different from mine and that much of what they were suggesting wouldn't work for me. I needed to find my own path to life-work harmony.

EVERYONE WILL DEAL with the life-work harmony issue in a different way, and that's okay. Don't let someone else tell you what you should focus on. Understand and acknowledge what *your* priorities are, then find ways to honour those priorities while getting other stuff done.

Even if you have set your priorities by choosing a couple of areas to focus on, it is still not easy. This is particularly true if you are a perfectionist. You have to let go of that need for perfection.

Accept that the superwoman who climbs the corporate ladder while being supermom and the perfect spouse doesn't exist. We cannot be all things to all people at the same time, and you have to be willing to let some things go or put them on hold for a while. There is a good chance that you will be able to get back to those interests at a future period in your life. For example, once my daughter went away to university, I was able to spend time on other areas of interest.

For those who do not have children, other things may become priorities through your life journey, such as caring for an ill or disabled partner, attending to your own health issues, caring for older parents or family members, or volunteering. Whatever you decide to focus on, be sure to set aside some time for self-care, whether this is a physical activity, doing something positive for your mental health, or spending time on something you really enjoy. It doesn't necessarily have to be a large amount of time so long as it is a period where you can disconnect from your responsibilities to others. If you don't look after yourself, you won't be much use to anyone else.

BELIEVE IN
YOURSELF

———————————

HUMILITY AND
SELF-PROMOTION

GROWING UP, MY siblings and I were taught to be humble. It wasn't okay to talk about our achievements, whether they were in the classroom or on the sports field. Rather, if people noticed our achievements and congratulated us for them, we would brush off or diminish their praise, or just quietly thank them.

This humbleness may have been helpful in the early stages of my career, as I was so extremely grateful for being able to enter such an exciting industry. However, I had to learn self-promotion skills to survive and advance in the oil and gas industry. When you are among a group of people who are good at extolling their virtues, you can get lost in the crowd if you do not learn to promote yourself.

Perhaps the first time I understood that some promotion was necessary was when I ran for a position on the board of my professional association. We had to prepare a short biography of our education and qualifications. After reading mine, a female landman came up to me and said, "Oh my gosh, I didn't realize how qualified you are." She was married to a well-known fellow landman who was heavily involved with the same association, and her comments made me realize that I needed to do more self-promotion, particularly if I was in the running for a new position or advancement in my organization. I learned that if I didn't speak up for myself, it was likely no one else would.

I sometimes still have difficulty promoting myself. I was recently at a breakfast meeting of the Calgary chapter of the Institute of Corporate Directors. As I usually try to do at functions like this, I sat beside someone I didn't know in order to expand my network. On my other side was a colleague I had known for a number of years.

Over breakfast, I talked with the gentleman I had just met about my work and board experience, and in turn I learned about his experiences. We stopped talking when the educational portion of the event began, but after the session ended, I gave him my business card and mentioned that I had published two books about the oil and gas industry. I told him they were written for the layperson and that one was about land rights and the other was about the exploration and production phases of the oil and gas industry. He said he would check them out.

The colleague sitting on my other side had overheard our conversation, and she stayed behind to speak with me after the event. "You should promote yourself more as a published author," she said. She pointed out that I had mentioned the books almost as an afterthought rather than talking about them as accomplishments.

I said in the introduction to this book that various people have called me a trailblazer. I don't necessarily promote myself as that, and perhaps I should do that more.

I THINK THAT many women walk a fine line between humility and self-promotion. If we are too humble, we can be viewed as mousy and we can miss out on opportunities. If we take self-promotion to the extreme, we can be viewed as being brash or a "bitch."

Many men are socialized to promote themselves and to talk about their accomplishments. Strong egos add to and support their self-promotion, and it can become a competition. If a woman is injected into this environment and has not been socialized in the same way, she will be lost in the group unless she finds her voice.

I'm not suggesting that you become boastful about your skills and accomplishments or embellish them, as some of your peers may do. Rather, I am suggesting that you quietly ensure that people know about your skills and interests. It is not always the loudest voice that gets all the attention, but you have to ensure that your voice is heard somewhere in the discussion.

It is good to remain humble, but don't let that stop you from promoting yourself if the opportunity presents itself. Sometimes the push you need is to ask yourself, "If I don't speak up, can I live with the consequences? What is the worst thing that could happen if I do speak up, and can I deal with that?"

Find your voice and become comfortable with promoting your skills and yourself. You don't have to do it the same way that men do. Find your own path.

CONFIDENCE AND SELF-ESTEEM

TRADITIONALLY, IN MY family culture as I was growing up, it wasn't unusual to see women with a poor self-image and low self-esteem. The high school I attended had a large population of Chinese students due to its proximity to Calgary's Chinatown. Many of the girls from this neighbourhood were very, very timid.

Growing up in a culture where males are valued more than females certainly doesn't help a young woman's self-esteem. I have a vivid memory of driving down to San Francisco along the Pacific coast to visit one of my mom's aunts. We stopped in Vancouver to pick up my paternal grandmother and my aunt, who is almost three years older than me, so our white station wagon was quite full. My dad, my mom, and I think my youngest brother were in the front seat, my two other brothers and my grandmother were in the middle seat, and my aunt and I sat in the back along with the luggage and food my grandmother insisted on bringing, including rice and a pot to cook it in so we could avoid having to eat in costly restaurants along the way. There may have been seat belts for the bench seats, but there were definitely no seats or seat belts in that back section.

I don't recall how many days it took for us to drive from Calgary to Vancouver to San Francisco, but I do remember meeting our relatives for the first time. My parents made introductions of "our number-one son," "our number-two son," and "our number-three son." Then, almost as an afterthought, they said, "These are the girls."

I could have become the meek, obedient Asian daughter. Instead I took the attitude that I would show them that they were wrong—that females are just as valuable and important as males. The rest, as they say, is history.

I believe that one of the greatest gifts a person can offer someone is to help them develop self-esteem, so I was determined to help my daughter develop high self-esteem as she was growing up. Giving her simple and then more difficult tasks to complete helped build her confidence. Even though she knew that she had skills to tackle problems, she needed constant reinforcement about her competencies until she internalized them and believed them herself.

I wasn't too concerned about her having too high a level of self-esteem or too much confidence in her abilities as she was growing up. I figured that life experiences would knock down her confidence and self-esteem somewhat as she encountered greater challenges. As she moved into young adulthood, I knew that I would need to continue to provide positive reinforcement. It also helped to remind her of past experiences when she persevered as she battled challenges and accomplished her goals.

— WISDOM GAINED —

I HAVE SEEN many women come into the business environment with low expectations of what they can achieve.
When a lack of confidence is coupled with the inherent
biases in the oil and gas industry, the prospects of suc-
ceeding in this industry can seem daunting. However, I
encourage these women to persevere.

Work on developing a high level of self-esteem and
confidence in your abilities. If necessary, start out by accom-
plishing small tasks and then move on to larger challenges.

Make sure that your self-talk contains positive mes-
sages to reinforce your confidence in yourself. You have
control of your self-esteem—how you view yourself. Watch
the negative self-talk to make sure it does not diminish
you as a person. Perhaps some of your behaviours need
an adjustment, but this does not diminish your value or
worth as a person.

If you are fortunate to already have high self-esteem
and confidence in your abilities, consider helping another
individual develop their own. While it can be a long process
and it can be frustrating to watch someone slip back to
negative, self-deprecating ways, it is very rewarding when
you see someone blossom and develop the confidence to
take control of their lives.

PARTING

THOUGHTS

'VE SPENT MY career in the oil and gas industry, but much of what I have learned could apply to other male-dominated fields. My observation from the periphery is that the financial and consumer products industries have been very good at supporting women and promoting them to upper management and executive levels. Other professions, such as in the legal and medical sectors, seem to struggle when it comes to promoting women to leadership. These observations are, of course, generalizations. In any industry, I am sure you can find companies and individuals that actively support and promote women to leadership roles... if you search hard enough.

While a few women have managed to break into the executive bastions—and they are to be congratulated for this—the male-dominated status quo has been painfully slow to change. "For two decades we have talked about pipelines, in the context of the number of women whose careers are progressing according to a certain trajectory," wrote Deborah Yedlin in the *Calgary Herald* (December 28, 2017). "The more women in that pipeline, the better the odds more make it into the C-suite—the offices of CEOs, CFOs, COOs and other senior execs. But that's not happening. Women are still self-selecting out."

Perhaps this is due to the family pressures and the multiple roles that many women are required to perform.

Or perhaps some women are recognizing that the costs associated with moving into those upper levels far outweigh the benefits. The increase in status, pay, and responsibility may not compensate enough for the increased time commitment, stress, and negative impact on health and relationships. Maybe they are content with the level that they are working at because it provides the flexibility and time they need to pursue other priorities, such as family, community service, or hobbies such as travel. Not everyone aspires to move into the executive level, and that should be okay. We should be sure that the women we are seeking to promote are striving for leadership positions in whichever industry we are speaking about.

But if, after considering the costs and benefits, you decide that scrambling to a higher-level position is a choice you want to make, then I say go for it with all of your energy and passion.

And if you are a woman who has already "made it," think about how you can support other exceptional women who are still struggling to get to where you are. Sometimes just that little bit of help and inspiration goes a long way.

That is what I have tried to do with this book. It is only now, looking back at my journey in the oil and gas industry, that I can appreciate how the gems of wisdom I picked up along the way have formed quite a collection, and I hope that they can help other women undertaking a similar journey. Not every gem is appropriate for every day. You have to choose the ones that suit a particular situation on a particular day.

As my journey has shown all too well, it's been a challenge for women to progress in the oil and gas industry, and many barriers remain. But we're making progress, and we need to keep going. Women have a lot to contribute.

ACKNOWLEDGMENTS

TO JESSE FINKELSTEIN and the team at Page Two Strategies, thank you for your understanding, support, and guidance. Your collective wisdom has made the process of publishing a book in the "memoir" category less painful than I originally anticipated.

In particular, I'd like to specially acknowledge my editor, Lana Okerlund. Your ability to smooth those rough passages and collect my thoughts into tight crystals helped me to convey my gems of wisdom more effectively. You did all this while still allowing my voice to come through and shine.

Additional special acknowledgment goes to Peter Cocking for your creative layout and design. It's always a pleasure to see what idea gems you come up with.

To my family, thank you for pushing me to achieve.

Finally, I'm grateful to all of the people I had the pleasure to work with through my career journey. Thank you for helping me learn the lessons I have learned.

KIRSTEY JANE

ABOUT THE AUTHOR

EVONNE LOUIE IS a recently retired oil and gas professional with almost forty years of experience in negotiations, government relations, business development, strategy development, mediation, and coaching. She has a Master of Business Administration, a Bachelor of Commerce, and a Bachelor of Science, all from the University of Calgary. She has been a member of the Canadian Association of Petroleum Landmen (CAPL) since 1980, was granted the Professional Landman designation in 1990, served three terms on the board of CAPL, and received CAPL's Special Recognition Award in 2015. A graduate of the Directors Education Program of the Institute of Corporate Directors, Ms. Louie was granted the ICD.D designation in 2011. She currently serves as a board member of the Calgary Convention Centre Authority and is a public member on the council of the College of Physicians and Surgeons of Alberta.

www.levonnelouie.com